WHY WE CAN'T WAIT

WHY WE CAN'T WAIT

MARTIN LUTHER KING, JR.

BEACON PRESS

BOSTON

Beacon Press
25 Beacon Street
Boston, Massachusetts 02108-2892

Beacon Press books are published under the auspices of the
Unitarian Universalist Association of Congregations. Beacon Press
gratefully acknowledges the Unitarian Universalist Veatch Program
at Shelter Rock for its generous support of the King Legacy series.

In Association With

This edition of *Why We Can't Wait* is based on an earlier edition,
published in the United States in 1963. Some spelling and punctuation
have been adjusted, and obvious errors have been corrected.
Printed in the United States of America

20   19   18   8   7   6   5   4 (pb)

20   19   18   8   7   6   5   4   3   2 (hc)

Library of Congress Cataloging in Publication Data
King, Martin Luther, Jr., 1929–1968.
Why we can't wait / Martin Luther King, Jr.
p. cm.
Originally published: New York : Harper & Row, 1964.
Includes bibliographical references and index.
ISBN 978-0-8070-0114-1 (hardcover. : alk. paper)
ISBN 978-0-8070-0112-7 (pbk. : alk. paper)
1. African Americans—Civil rights. 2. African Americans—
Civil rights—Alabama—Birmingham. 3. United States—Race relations.
4. Birmingham (Ala.)—Race relations. I. Title.
E185.61.K54 2010
323.1196'0730761781—dc22   2010027828

FRONT COVER: Dr. King walks to a press conference on May 16, 1963,
in Birmingham. To King's right is Rev. Ralph Abernathy.
The other men are unidentified. (Bettman/Corbis)
BACK COVER: A seventeen-year-old demonstrator is
set upon by dogs in Birmingham on May 3, 1963. He was in
defiance of an "anti-parade" ordinance. (AP/Wide World)

TO MY CHILDREN

Yolanda—Martin III—Dexter—Bernice
for whom I dream that one day soon
they will no longer be judged by the color of
their skin but by the content of their character

I acknowledge with affection and gratitude
the help of Hermine I. Popper, whose
perception and intelligence enabled her to
do a constructive and important editorial job.

I am also grateful to Alfred Duckett for his efforts
and suggestions in the early stages of my manuscript.

CONTENTS

INTRODUCTION

In 1963, Birmingham was often called the most segregated city in America. Our freedom struggle there
revealed how brutal and pervasive the segregation pattern was and how challenging and difficult this part of
our journey would be. The more we demanded our
rights as citizens, the more hatred and violence we en-
countered from segregationist public officials. Despite
the intense opposition, however, hundreds of Birmingham citizens joined the struggle to bring about change.
Marching for freedom and submitting to jailing became
an ordinary daily event. But there came a time when
the jails were full, even when police started to confine
other arrested protesters in the local fairground.

It was Good Friday, and there was a church full of
people waiting to march for freedom with Dr. Martin Luther King, Jr., leading them. Their objectives
included the elimination of Birmingham's rigid segregation. They wanted the right to vote. They wanted
jobs and the ability to try on clothes in all the places
where they shopped. They wanted public schools
opened to all children without regard to the color of
their skin. Even in the liquor stores African Americans

were required to form a separate waiting line in order to be served. Still we continued to sing, "We would not let anything turn us around," as one of our popular freedom songs intoned.

With this backdrop, I was there when Martin faced his most poignant decision in the midst of the Birmingham struggle. The jails were full, and protestors were awaiting bail, but we were out of money. In room 30 of the A. G. Gaston Motel, there was a long and a very intense meeting that brought together local Birmingham civic leaders with Dr. King and his Southern Christian Leadership Conference (S.C.L.C.) team. All of us had responded to the call from the Reverend Fred Shuttlesworth, the local civil rights leader who had invited Dr. King to Birmingham. With a church full of people waiting for Dr. King to lead another peaceful march through the downtown area, we had to determine. We had called a boycott to bring attention to the reason for our struggle, because we wanted the business community to understand the goals of our movement.

In this book, Martin recalls his experience of heartfelt despair as he quietly listened to the heated arguments about whether he should concentrate on raising money that would be used to bail out the hundreds of people already incarcerated or should go to jail himself, as he had urged so many others to do just that—not only in Birmingham but in hotbeds of protest activity in other cities.

I still cry as I read about the agony he felt as he listened to all of us in room 30. Most of us urged him to stay out of jail at this point because of the urgent need for bail money. Martin recalled that there were "twenty-four pairs of eyes" upon him. At that moment, he had *"come face to face with himself"* as leader. After all, he had encouraged people from across the community to accept suffering, to accept jailing. It would not be only the eyes of the people of Birmingham on him but the eyes and ears of people nationwide. He was *"alone in that crowded room."*

After enduring his silent agony, he communicated in no uncertain terms that he had made his decision. Without saying anything, he stood up and walked into the adjoining bedroom. When he reentered the parlor where we were gathered, he had put on his marching clothes. We could see that there was no longer a need to ponder his choices. Words could not have communicated more powerfully that he had made his decision. The debate was over.

He later explained that he "could not encourage hundreds of people to make a stunning sacrifice and then excuse himself." We stood, made a circle, and crossed and held hands, as was our custom, and sang "We Shall Overcome," the anthem of our movement. Some of us sang with tears in our eyes. It was a powerful moment.

Martin's decision to go to jail was a crucial turning point for the civil rights struggle. Although he was placed in solitary confinement, his spirit was lifted when his lawyers were finally allowed to visit him. Clarence Jones brought the encouraging news that Harry Belafonte had been able to raise fifty thousand dollars for bail bonds. Those of us who participated in that argument in room 30 of the Gaston Motel realized that Martin had made the right decision, both morally and tactically.

While in jail Martin would write his most profound explanation of our nonviolent strategy. His now well-known "Letter from Birmingham Jail" was a response to a group of white Birmingham clergymen who severely criticized him as an outside agitator. Martin's detailed defense can be summarized in the poetic line "Injustice anywhere is a threat to justice everywhere."

Soon the whole country and indeed the whole world would take note of our work in Birmingham, our determination to be free. In this book, Dr. King explains, in the clearest way I've ever heard, how nonviolence—"The Sword that Heals"—can become a powerful tool to transform, and thereby to transform systems designed to abuse people. He explains how all African Americans involved in our own liberation struggle came to embody the dignity of moral conviction and self-sacrifice. Importantly, he explains here how the way of nonviolence heals the oppressed as well as the oppressor. Rather than simply expressing hurt, anger, and victimhood, oppressed people can experience the healing necessary for bringing about the Beloved Community. It had indeed been "Bull Connor's Birmingham," but with Martin King, Jr., and Fred Shuttlesworth and other committed people working together, there emerged "A New Day in Birmingham."

Another "tool" Dr. King describes in this book is the importance of freedom songs. He shows how and why the songs were "the soul of the movement," explaining that they are more than just "incantations of clever phrases," but also "adaptations of the songs the slaves sang."

We learned some important lessons in our Birmingham struggle, and we need to apply those lessons now. As Martin said, "We can't wait." We cannot wait, because the jails are full of young black men, including many who are fathers but unable to parent their children. We can't wait, because we know now that failing to make education a priority cheats the country of latent talent. We can't wait, because our young men and women are being programmed to kill (it's called "serving our country").

None of this is to suggest that the road ahead will be easy. The Birmingham struggle was difficult. But I remember something a white Birmingham businessman told me many years after the events recounted in this book. Mr. Emil Hess had the courage to acknowledge that Birmingham had catapulted America into the twentieth century.

If we heed Martin Luther King's call today, we can launch a struggle that can catapult our nation into a new century of even more exciting progress toward the ideal of peace with social justice.

Dorothy F. Cotton

INTRODUCTION

It is the beginning of the year of our Lord 1963.

I see a young Negro boy. He is sitting on a stoop in front of a vermin-infested apartment house in Harlem. The stench of garbage is in the halls. The drunks, the jobless, the junkies are shadow figures of his everyday world. The boy goes to a school attended mostly by Negro students with a scattering of Puerto Ricans. His father is one of the jobless. His mother is a sleep-in domestic, working for a family on Long Island.

I see a young Negro girl. She is sitting on the stoop of a rickety wooden one-family house in Birmingham. Some visitors would call it a shack. It needs paint badly and the patched-up roof appears in danger of caving in. Half a dozen small children, in various stages of undress, are scampering about the house. The girl is forced to play the role of their mother. She can no longer attend the all-Negro school in her neighborhood because her mother died only recently after a car accident. Neighbors say if the ambulance hadn't come so late to take her to the all-Negro hospital the mother might still be alive. The girl's father is a porter in a downtown department store. He will always be a porter, for there are no promotions for the Negro in this store, where every counter serves him except the one that sells hot dogs and orange juice.

This boy and this girl, separated by stretching miles, are wondering: Why does misery constantly haunt the Negro? In some distant past, had their forebears done some tragic injury to the nation, and was the curse of punishment upon the black race? Had they shirked in their duty as patriots, betrayed their country, denied their national birthright? Had they refused to defend their land against a foreign foe?

Not all of history is recorded in the books supplied to school children in Harlem or Birmingham. Yet this boy and this girl know something of the part of history which has been censored by the white writers and purchasers of board-of-education books. They know that Negroes were with George Washington at Valley Forge. They know that the first American to shed blood in the revolution which freed his country from British oppression was a black seaman named Crispus Attucks. The boy's Sunday-school teacher has told him that one of the team who designed the capital of their nation, Washington, D.C., was a Negro, Benjamin Banneker. Once the girl had heard a speaker, invited to her school during Negro History Week. This speaker told how, for two hundred years, without wages, black people, brought to this land in slave ships and in chains, had drained the swamps, built the homes, made cotton king and helped, on whiplashed backs, to lift this nation from colonial obscurity to commanding influence in domestic commerce and world trade.

Wherever there was hard work, dirty work, dangerous work—in the mines, on the docks, in the blistering foundries—Negroes had done more than their share.

The pale history books in Harlem and Birmingham told how the nation had fought a war over slavery. Abraham Lincoln had signed a document that would come to be known as the Emancipation Proclamation. The war had been won but not a just peace. Equality had never arrived. Equality was a hundred years late.

The boy and the girl knew more than history. They knew something about current events. They knew that African nations had burst the bonds of colonialism. They knew that a great-great-grandson of Crispus Attucks might be ruled out of some restricted, all-white restaurant in some restricted, all-white section of a southern town, his United States Marines uniform notwithstanding. They knew that Negroes living in the capital of their own nation were confined to ghettos and could not always get a job for which they were qualified. They knew that white supremacists had defied the Supreme Court and that southern governors had attempted to interpose themselves between the people and the highest law of the land. They knew that, for years, their own lawyers had won great victories in the courts which were not being translated into reality.

They were seeing on television, hearing from the radio, reading in the newspapers that this was the one-hundredth birthday of their freedom.

But freedom had a dull ring, a mocking emptiness when, in their time—in the short life span of this boy and girl—buses had stopped rolling in Montgomery; sit-inners were jailed and beaten; freedom riders were brutalized and mobbed; dogs' fangs were bared in Birmingham; and in Brooklyn, New York, there were certain kinds of construction jobs for whites only.

It was the summer of 1963. Was emancipation a fact? Was freedom a force?

The boy in Harlem stood up. The girl in Birmingham arose. Separated by stretching miles, both of them squared their shoulders and lifted their eyes toward heaven. Across the miles they joined hands, and took a firm, forward step. It was a step that rocked the richest, most powerful nation to its foundations.

This is the story of that boy and that girl. This is the story of *Why We Can't Wait.*

MARTIN LUTHER KING, JR.
Atlanta, Georgia
January 1964

I

The Negro Revolution—
Why 1963?

The bitterly cold winter of 1962 lingered throughout
the opening months of 1963, touching the land with
chill and frost, and then was replaced by a placid spring.
Americans awaited a quiet summer. That it would be
pleasant they had no doubt. The worst of it would
be the nightmare created by sixty million cars, all apparently trying to reach the same destination at the
same time. Fifty million families looked forward to
the pleasure of two hundred million vacations in the
American tradition of the frenetic hunt for relaxation.

It would be a pleasant summer because, in the mind
of the average man, there was little cause for concern.
The blithe outlook about the state of the nation was
reflected from as high up as the White House. The administration confidently readied a tax-reduction bill.
Business and employment were at comfortable levels.
Money was—for many Americans—plentiful.

Summer came, and the weather was beautiful. But
the climate, the social climate of American life, erupted
into lightning flashes, trembled with thunder and vi-
brated to the relentless, growing rain of protest come

to life through the land. Explosively, America's third revolution—the Negro Revolution—had begun.

For the first time in the long and turbulent history of the nation, almost one thousand cities were engulfed in civil turmoil, with violence trembling just below the surface. Reminiscent of the French Revolution of 1789, the streets had become a battleground, just as they had become the battleground, in the 1830s, of England's tumultuous Chartist movement. As in these two revolutions, a submerged social group, propelled by a burning need for justice, lifting itself with sudden swiftness, moving with determination and a majestic scorn for risk and danger, created an uprising so powerful that it shook a huge society from its comfortable base.

Never in American history had a group seized the streets, the squares, the sacrosanct business thoroughfares and the marbled halls of government to protest and proclaim the unendurability of their oppression. Had room-size machines turned human, burst from the plants that housed them and stalked the land in revolt, the nation could not have been more amazed. Undeniably, the Negro had been an object of sympathy and wore the scars of deep grievances, but the nation had come to count on him as a creature who could quietly endure, silently suffer and patiently wait. He was well trained in service and, whatever the provocation, he neither pushed back nor spoke back.

Just as lightning makes no sound until it strikes, the Negro Revolution generated quietly. But when it struck, the revealing flash of its power and the impact of its sincerity and fervor displayed a force of a frightening intensity. Three hundred years of humiliation, abuse and deprivation cannot be expected to find voice in a whisper. The storm clouds did not release a "gentle rain from heaven," but a whirlwind, which has not yet spent its force or attained its full momentum.

Because there is more to come; because American society is bewildered by the spectacle of the Negro in revolt; because the dimensions are vast and the implications deep in a nation with twenty million Negroes, it is important to understand the history that is being made today.

II

Some years ago, I sat in a Harlem department store, surrounded by hundreds of people. I was autographing copies of *Stride Toward Freedom*, my book about the Montgomery bus boycott of 1955–56. As I signed my name to a page, I felt something sharp plunge forcefully into my chest. I had been stabbed with a letter opener, struck home by a woman who would later be judged insane. Rushed by ambulance to Harlem Hospital, I lay in a bed for hours while preparations were made to remove the keen-edged knife from my body. Days later, when I was well enough to talk with Dr. Aubrey Maynard, the chief of the surgeons who performed the delicate, dangerous operation, I learned the reason for the long delay that preceded surgery. He told me that the razor tip of the instrument had been touching my aorta and that my whole chest had to be opened to extract it.

"If you had sneezed during all those hours of waiting," Dr. Maynard said, "your aorta would have been punctured and you would have drowned in your own blood."

In the summer of 1963 the knife of violence was just that close to the nation's aorta. Hundreds of cities might now be mourning countless dead but for the operation of certain forces which gave political surgeons an opportunity to cut boldly and safely to remove the deadly peril.

What was it that gave us the second chance? To answer this we must answer another question. Why did this Revolution occur in 1963? Negroes had for decades endured evil. In the words of the poet, they had long asked: "Why must the blackness of nighttime collect in our mouth; why must we always taste grief in our blood?" Any time would seem to have been the right time. Why 1963?

Why did a thousand cities shudder almost simultaneously and why did the whole world—in gleaming capitals and mud-hut villages—hold its breath during those months? Why was it this year that the American Negro, so long ignored, so long written out of the pages of history books, tramped a declaration of freedom with his marching feet across the pages of newspapers, the television screens and the magazines? Sarah Turner closed the kitchen cupboard and went into the streets; John Wilkins shut down the elevator and enlisted in the nonviolent army; Bill Griggs slammed the brakes of his truck and slid to the sidewalk; the Reverend Arthur Jones led his flock into the streets and held church in jail. The words and actions of parliaments and statesmen, of kings and prime ministers, movie stars and athletes, were shifted from the front pages to make room for the history-making deeds of the servants, the drivers, the elevator operators and the ministers. Why in 1963, and what has this to do with why the dark threat of violence did not erupt in blood?

III

The Negro had been deeply disappointed over the slow pace of school desegregation. He knew that in 1954 the highest court in the land had handed down a decree calling for desegregation of schools "with all deliberate speed." He knew that this edict from the Supreme Court had been heeded with all deliberate delay. At the beginning of 1963, nine years after this historic decision, approximately 9 percent of southern Negro students were attending integrated schools. If this pace were maintained, it would be the year 2054 before integration in southern schools would be a reality.

In its wording the Supreme Court decision had revealed an awareness that attempts would be made to evade its intent. The phrase "all deliberate speed" did not mean that another century should be allowed to unfold before we released Negro children from the narrow pigeonhole of the segregated schools; it meant that, giving some courtesy and consideration to the need for softening old attitudes and outdated customs, democracy must press ahead, out of the past of ignorance and intolerance, and into the present of educational opportunity and moral freedom.

Yet the statistics make it abundantly clear that the segregationists of the South remained undefeated by the decision. From every section of Dixie, the announcement of the high court had been met with declarations of defiance. Once recovered from their initial outrage, these defenders of the status quo had seized the offensive to impose their own schedule of change. The progress that was supposed to have been achieved with deliberate speed had created change for less than 2 percent of Negro children in most areas of the South and not even one-tenth of 1 percent in some parts of the deepest South.

There was another factor in the slow pace of progress, a factor of which few are aware and even fewer understand. It is an unadvertised fact that soon after the 1954 decision the Supreme Court retreated from its own position by giving approval to the Pupil Placement Law. This law permitted the states themselves to determine where school children might be placed by virtue of family background, special ability and other subjective criteria. The Pupil Placement Law was almost as far-reaching in modifying and limiting the integration of schools as the original decision had been in attempting to eliminate segregation. Without technically reversing itself, the Court had granted legal sanction to tokenism and thereby guaranteed that segregation, in substance, would last for an indefinite period, though formally it was illegal.

In order, then, to understand the deep disillusion of the Negro in 1963, one must examine his contrasting emotions at the time of the decision and during the nine years that followed. One must understand the pendulum swing between the elation that arose when the edict was handed down and the despair that followed the failure to bring it to life.

A second reason for the outburst in 1963 was rooted

in disappointment with both political parties. From the city of Los Angeles in 1960, the Democratic party had written an historic and sweeping civil-rights pronouncement into its campaign platform. The Democratic standard bearer had repeated eloquently and often that the moral weight of the presidency must be applied to this burning issue. From Chicago, the Republican party had been generous in its convention vows on civil rights, although its candidate had made no great effort in his campaign to convince the nation that he would redeem his party's promises.

Then 1961 and 1962 arrived, with both parties marking time in the cause of justice. In the Congress, reactionary Republicans were still doing business with the Dixiecrats. And the feeling was growing among Negroes that the administration had oversimplified and underestimated the civil-rights issue. President Kennedy, if not backing down, had backed away from a key pledge of his campaign—to wipe out housing discrimination immediately "with the stroke of a pen." When he had finally signed the housing order, two years after taking office, its terms, though praiseworthy, had revealed a serious weakness in its failure to attack the key problem of discrimination in financing by banks and other institutions.

While Negroes were being appointed to some significant jobs, and social hospitality was being extended at the White House to Negro leaders, the dreams of the masses remained in tatters. The Negro felt that he recognized the same old bone that had been tossed to him in the past—only now it was being handed to him on a platter, with courtesy.

The administration had fashioned its primary approach to discrimination in the South around a series of lawsuits chiefly designed to protect the right to vote. Opposition toward action on other fronts had begun to harden. With each new Negro protest, we were advised, sometimes privately and sometimes in public, to call off our efforts and channel all of our energies into registering voters. On each occasion we would agree with the importance of voting rights, but would patiently seek to explain that Negroes did not want to neglect all other rights while one was selected for concentrated attention.

It was necessary to conclude that our argument was not persuading the administration any more than the government's logic was prevailing with us. Negroes had manifested their faith by racking up a substantial majority of their votes for President Kennedy. They had expected more of him than of the previous administration. In no sense had President Kennedy betrayed his promises. Yet his administration appeared to believe it was doing as much as was politically possible and had, by its positive deeds, earned enough credit to coast on civil rights. Politically, perhaps, this was not a surprising conclusion. How many people understood, during the first two years of the Kennedy administration, that the Negroes' "Now" was becoming as militant as the segregationists' "Never"? Eventually the president would set political considerations aside and rise to the level of his own unswerving moral commitment. But this was still in the future.

No discussion of the influences that bore on the

thinking of the Negro in 1963 would be complete without some attention to the relationship of this Revolution to international events. Throughout the upheavals of cold-war politics, Negroes had seen their government go to the brink of nuclear conflict more than once. The justification for risking the annihilation of the human race was always expressed in terms of America's willingness to go to any lengths to preserve freedom. To the Negro that readiness for heroic measures in the defense of liberty disappeared or became tragically weak when the threat was within our own borders and was concerned with the Negro's liberty. While the Negro is not so selfish as to stand isolated in concern for his own dilemma, ignoring the ebb and flow of events around the world, there is a certain bitter irony in the picture of his country championing freedom in foreign lands and failing to ensure that freedom to twenty million of its own.

From beyond the borders of his own land, the Negro had been inspired by another powerful force. He had watched the decolonization and liberation of nations in Africa and Asia since World War II. He knew that yellow, black and brown people had felt for years that the American Negro was too passive, unwilling to take strong measures to gain his freedom. He might have remembered the visit to this country of an African head of state, who was called upon by a delegation of prominent American Negroes. When they began reciting to him their long list of grievances, the visiting statesman had waved a weary hand and said:

"I am aware of current events. I know everything

you are telling me about what the white man is doing to the Negro. Now tell me: What is the Negro doing for himself?"

The American Negro saw, in the land from which he had been snatched and thrown into slavery, a great pageant of political progress. He realized that just thirty years ago there were only three independent nations in the whole of Africa. He knew that by 1963 more than thirty-four African nations had risen from colonial bondage. The Negro saw black statesmen voting on vital issues in the United Nations—and knew that in many cities of his own land he was not permitted to take that significant walk to the ballot box. He saw black kings and potentates ruling from palaces—and knew he had been condemned to move from small ghettos to larger ones. Witnessing the drama of Negro progress elsewhere in the world, witnessing a level of conspicuous consumption at home exceeding anything in our history, it was natural that by 1963 Negroes would rise with resolution and demand a share of governing power, and living conditions measured by American standards rather than by the standards of colonial impoverishment.

An additional and decisive fact confronted the Negro and helped to bring him out of the houses, into the streets, out of the trenches and into the front lines. This was his recognition that one hundred years had passed since emancipation, with no profound effect on his plight.

With the dawn of 1963, plans were afoot all over the land to celebrate the Emancipation Proclamation, the one-hundredth birthday of the Negro's liberation from bondage. In Washington, a federal commission had been established to mark the event. Governors of states and mayors of cities had utilized the date to enhance their political image by naming commissions, receiving committees, issuing statements, planning state pageants, sponsoring dinners, endorsing social activities. Champagne, this year, would bubble on countless tables. Appropriately attired, over thick cuts of roast beef, legions would listen as luminous phrases were spun to salute the great democratic landmark which 1963 represented.

But alas! All the talk and publicity accompanying the centennial only served to remind the Negro that he still wasn't free, that he still lived a form of slavery disguised by certain niceties of complexity. As the then vice president, Lyndon B. Johnson, phrased it: "Emancipation was a Proclamation but not a fact." The pen of the Great Emancipator had moved the Negro into the sunlight of physical freedom, but actual conditions had left him behind in the shadow of political, psychological, social, economic and intellectual bondage. In the South, discrimination faced the Negro in its obvious and glaring forms. In the North, it confronted him in hidden and subtle disguise.

The Negro also had to recognize that one hundred years after emancipation he lived on a lonely island of economic insecurity in the midst of a vast ocean of material prosperity. Negroes are still at the bottom of the economic ladder. They live within two concentric circles of segregation. One imprisons them on the basis of color, while the other confines them within a separate culture of poverty. The average Negro is born into want and deprivation. His struggle to escape his circumstances is hindered by color discrimination. He is deprived of normal education and normal social and economic opportunities. When he seeks opportunity, he is told, in effect, to lift himself by his own boot-straps, advice which does not take into account the fact that he is barefoot.

By 1963, most of America's working population had forgotten the Great Depression or had never known it. The slow and steady growth of unemployment had touched some of the white working force but the pro-portion was still not more than one in twenty. This was not true for the Negro. There were two and one-half times as many jobless Negroes as whites in 1963, and their median income was half that of the white man. Many white Americans of good will have never connected bigotry with economic exploitation. They have deplored prejudice, but tolerated or ignored eco-nomic injustice. But the Negro knows that these two evils have a malignant kinship. He knows this because he has worked in shops that employ him exclusively because the pay is below a living standard. He knows it is not an accident of geography that wage rates in the South are significantly lower than those in the North. He knows that the spotlight recently focused on the growth in the number of women who work is not a phenomenon in Negro life. The average Negro woman has always had to work to help keep her family in food and clothes.

To the Negro, as 1963 approached, the economic structure of society appeared to be so ordered that a precise sifting of jobs took place. The lowest-paid employment and the most tentative jobs were reserved for him. If he sought to change his position, he was walled in by the tall barrier of discrimination. As summer came, more than ever the spread of unemployment had visible and tangible dimensions to the colored American. Equality meant dignity and dignity demanded a job that was secure and a paycheck that lasted throughout the week.

The Negro's economic problem was compounded by the emergence and growth of automation. Since discrimination and lack of education confined him to unskilled and semi-skilled labor, the Negro was and remains the first to suffer in these days of great technological development. The Negro knew all too well that there was not in existence the kind of vigorous retraining program that could really help him to grapple with the magnitude of his problem.

The symbol of the job beyond the great wall was construction work. The Negro whose slave labor helped to build a nation was being told by employers on the one hand and unions on the other that there was no place for him in this industry. Billions were being spent on city, state and national building for which the Negro paid taxes but could draw no paycheck. No one who saw the spanning bridges, the grand mansions, the sturdy docks and stout factories of the South could question the Negro's ability to build if he were given a chance for apprenticeship training. It was plain, hard, raw discrimination that shut him out of decent employment.

In 1963, the Negro, who had realized for many years that he was not truly free, awoke from a stupor of inaction with the cold dash of realization that 1963 meant one hundred years after Lincoln gave his autograph to the cause of freedom.

The milestone of the centennial of emancipation gave the Negro a reason to act—a reason so simple and obvious that he almost had to step back to see it.

Simple logic made it painfully clear that if this centennial were to be meaningful, it must be observed not as a celebration, but rather as a commemoration of the one moment in the country's history when a bold, brave *start* had been made, and a rededication to the obvious fact that urgent business was at hand—the resumption of that noble journey toward the goals reflected in the Preamble to the Constitution, the Constitution itself, the Bill of Rights and the Thirteenth, Fourteenth and Fifteenth Amendments.

Yet not all of these forces conjoined could have brought about the massive and largely bloodless Revolution of 1963 if there had not been at hand a philosophy and a method worthy of its goals. Nonviolent direct action did not originate in America, but it found its natural home in this land, where refusal to cooperate with injustice was an ancient and honorable tradition and where Christian forgiveness was written into the minds and hearts of good men. Tested in Montgomery during the winter of 1955-56, and toughened throughout the South in the eight ensuing years, nonviolent resistance had become, by 1963, the logical force in the greatest mass-action crusade for freedom that has ever occurred in American history.

Nonviolence is a powerful and just weapon. It is a weapon unique in history, which cuts without wounding and ennobles the man who wields it. It is a sword that heals. Both a practical and a moral answer to the Negro's cry for justice, nonviolent direct action proved that it could win victories without losing wars, and so became the triumphant tactic of the Negro Revolution of 1963.

II

The Sword That Heals

In the summer of 1963 a need and a time and a circumstance and the mood of a people came together. In order to understand the present Revolution, it is necessary to examine in more extensive detail the psychological and social conditions that produced it and the events that brought the philosophy and method of nonviolent direct action into the forefront of the struggle.

It is important to understand, first of all, that the Revolution is not indicative of a sudden loss of patience within the Negro. The Negro had never really been patient in the pure sense of the word. The posture of silent waiting was forced upon him psychologically because he was shackled physically.

In the days of slavery, this suppression was openly, scientifically and consistently applied. Sheer physical force kept the Negro captive at every point. He was prevented from learning to read and write, prevented by laws actually inscribed in the statute books. He was forbidden to associate with other Negroes living on the same plantation, except when weddings or funerals took place. Punishment for any form of resistance or complaint about his condition could range from mutilation to death. Families were torn apart, friends separated, cooperation to improve their condition carefully thwarted. Fathers and mothers were sold from their children and children were bargained away from their parents. Young girls were, in many cases, sold to become the breeders of fresh generations of slaves. The slaveholders of America had devised with almost scientific precision their systems for keeping the Negro defenseless, emotionally and physically.

With the ending of physical slavery after the Civil War, new devices were found to "keep the Negro in his place." It would take volumes to describe these methods, extending from birth in jim-crow hospitals through burial in jim-crow sections of cemeteries. They are too well known to require a catalogue here. Yet one of the revelations during the past few years is the fact that the straitjackets of race prejudice and discrimination do not wear only southern labels. The subtle, psychological technique of the North has approached in its ugliness and victimization of the Negro the outright terror and open brutality of the South. The result has been a demeanor that passed for patience in the eyes of the white man, but covered a powerful impatience in the heart of the Negro.

For years, in the South, the white segregationist has been saying the Negro was "satisfied." He has claimed "we get along beautifully with our Negroes because we understand them. We only have trouble when outside agitators come in and stir it up." Many expressed this point of view knowing that it was a lie of majestic proportions. Others believed they were speaking the truth. For corroboration, they would tell you: "Why, I talked to my cook and she said . . ." or, "I discussed this frankly with the colored boy who works for us and I told him to express himself freely. He said . . ."

White people in the South may never fully know the extent to which Negroes defended themselves and protected their jobs—and, in many cases, their lives— by perfecting an air of ignorance and agreement. In days gone by, no cook would have dared to tell her employer what he ought to know. She had to tell him what he wanted to hear. She knew that the penalty for speaking the truth could be loss of her job.

During the Montgomery bus boycott, a white family summoned their Negro cook and asked her if she supported the terrible things the Negroes were doing, boycotting buses and demanding jobs.

"Oh, no, ma'am, I won't have anything to do with that boycott thing," the cook said. "I am just going to stay away from the buses as long as that trouble is going on." No doubt she left a satisfied audience. But as she walked home from her job, on feet already weary from a full day's work, she walked proudly, knowing that she was marching with a movement that would bring into being nonsegregated bus travel in Montgomery.

Jailing the Negro was once as much of a threat as the loss of a job. To any Negro who displayed a spark of manhood, a southern law-enforcement officer could say: "Nigger, watch your step, or I'll put you in jail." The Negro knew what going to jail meant. It meant not only confinement and isolation from his loved ones. It meant that at the jailhouse he could probably expect a severe beating. And it meant that his day in court, if he had it, would be a mockery of justice.

Even today there still exists in the South—and in certain areas of the North—the license that our society allows to unjust officials who implement their authority in the name of justice to practice injustice against minorities. Where, in the days of slavery, social license and custom placed the unbridled power of the whip in the hands of overseers and masters, today—especially in the southern half of the nation—armies of officials are clothed in uniform, invested with authority, armed with the instruments of violence and death and conditioned to believe that they can intimidate, maim or kill Negroes with the same recklessness that once motivated the slaveowner. If one doubts this conclusion, let him search the records and find how rarely in any southern state a police officer has been punished for abusing a Negro.

Since nonviolent action has entered the scene, however, the white man has gasped at a new phenomenon. He has seen Negroes, by the hundreds and by the thousands, marching toward him, knowing they are going to jail, wanting to go to jail, willing to accept the confinement, willing to risk the beatings and the uncertain justice of the southern courts.

There were no more powerful moments in the Birmingham episode than during the closing days of the campaign, when Negro youngsters ran after white policemen, asking to be locked up. There was an element of unmalicious mischief in this. The Negro youngsters, although perfectly willing to submit to imprisonment, knew that we had already filled up the jails, and that the police had no place left to take them.

When, for decades, you have been able to make a

man compromise his manhood by threatening him with a cruel and unjust punishment, and when suddenly he turns upon you and says: "Punish me. I do not deserve it. But because I do not deserve it, I will accept it so that the world will know that I am right and you are wrong," you hardly know what to do. You feel defeated and secretly ashamed. You know that this man is as good a man as you are; that from some mysterious source he has found the courage and the conviction to meet physical force with soul force.

So it was that, to the Negro, going to jail was no longer a disgrace but a badge of honor. The Revolution of the Negro not only attacked the external cause of his misery, but revealed him to himself. He was *somebody*. He had a sense of *somebodiness*. He was *impatient* to be free.

In the past decade, still another technique had begun to replace the old methods for thwarting the Negroes' dreams and aspirations. This is the method known as "tokenism." The dictionary interprets the word "token" in the following manner: "A symbol. Indication, evidence, as a token of friendship, a keepsake. A piece of metal used in place of a coin, as for paying carfare on conveyances operated by those who sell the tokens. A sign, a mark, emblem, memorial, omen."

When the Supreme Court modified its decision on school desegregation by approving the Pupil Placement Law, it permitted tokenism to corrupt its intent. It meant that Negroes could be handed the glitter of metal symbolizing the true coin, and authorizing a short-term trip toward democracy. But he who sells you the token instead of the coin always retains the power to revoke its worth, and to command you to get off the bus before you have reached your destination. Tokenism is a promise to pay. Democracy, in its finest sense, is payment.

The Negro wanted to feel pride in his race? With tokenism, the solution was simple. If all twenty million Negroes would keep looking at Ralph Bunche, the one man in so exalted a post would generate such a volume of pride that it could be cut into portions and served to everyone. A judge here and a judge there; an executive behind a polished desk in a carpeted office; a high government administrator with a toehold on a cabinet post; one student in a Mississippi university lofted there by an army; three Negro children admitted to the whole high-school system of a major city—all these were tokens used to obscure the persisting reality of segregation and discrimination.

For a decade the hard struggles had culminated in limited gains, which, if they advanced at all, crawled sluggishly forward. Schools, jobs, housing, voting rights and political positions—in each of these areas, manipulation with tokenism was the rule. Negroes had begun to feel that a policy was crystallizing, that all their struggles had brought them merely to a new level in which a selected few would become educated, honored and integrated to represent and substitute for the many.

Those who argue in favor of tokenism point out that we must begin somewhere; that it is unwise to spurn any breakthrough, no matter how limited. This position has a certain validity, and the Negro freedom movement has more often than not attained broad victories which had small beginnings. There is a critical distinction, however, between a modest start and tokenism. The tokenism Negroes condemn is recognizable because it is an end in itself. Its purpose is not to begin a process, but instead to end the process of protest and pressure. It is a hypocritical gesture, not a constructive first step.

I have gone into the Negro's resentment of tokenism at some length for I believe that analyzing his feelings about it will help to elucidate the uncompromising position he takes today. I think it will explain why he believes that half a loaf is no bread. I think it will justify his conviction that he must not turn back.

As I write, at the end of the first long season of Revolution, the Negro is not unmindful of or indifferent to the progress that has already been made. He notes with approval the radical change in the administration's approach to civil rights, and the small but visible gains being made on various fronts across the country. If he is still saying, "Not enough," it is because he does not feel that he should be expected to be *grateful* for the halting and inadequate attempts of his society to catch up with the basic rights he ought to have inherited automatically, centuries ago, by virtue of his membership in the human family and his American birthright.

In this conviction, he subscribes to the words of President Kennedy, uttered on June 11, 1963, only a few months before his tragic death: "We are confronted primarily with a moral issue. It is as old as the Scriptures and is as clear as the American Constitution. The heart of the question is whether all Americans are to be afforded equal rights and equal opportunities . . . Those who do nothing are inviting shame as well as violence. Those who act boldly are recognizing right as well as reality."

II

For a hundred years since emancipation, Negroes had searched for the elusive path to freedom. They knew that they had to fashion a body of tactics suitable for their unique and special conditions. The words of the Constitution had declared them free, but life had told them that they were a twice-burdened people—they lived in the lowest stratum of society, and within it they were additionally imprisoned by a caste of color.

For decades the long and winding trails led to dead ends. Booker T. Washington, in the dark days that followed Reconstruction, advised them: "Let down your buckets where you are." Be content, he said in effect, with doing well what the times permit you to do at all. However, this path, they soon felt, had too little freedom in its present and too little promise in its future.

Dr. W.E.B. Du Bois, in his earlier years at the turn of the century, urged the "talented tenth" to rise and pull behind it the mass of the race. His doctrine served somewhat to counteract the apparent resignation of Booker T. Washington's philosophy. Yet, in the very nature of Du Bois's outlook there was no role for the whole people. It was a tactic for an aristocratic elite who would themselves be benefited while leaving behind the "untalented" 90 percent.

After the First World War, Marcus Garvey made an appeal to the race that had the virtue of rejecting concepts of inferiority. He called for a return to Africa and a resurgence of race pride. His movement attained mass dimensions, and released a powerful emotional response because it touched a truth which had long been dormant in the mind of the Negro. There was reason to be proud of their heritage as well as of their bitterly won achievements in America. Yet his plan was doomed because an exodus to Africa in the twentieth century by a people who had struck roots for three and a half centuries in the New World did not have the ring of progress.

With the death of the Garvey movement, the way opened for the development of the doctrine which held the center of the stage for almost thirty years. This was the doctrine, consistently championed and ably conducted by the National Association for the Advancement of Colored People, that placed its reliance on the Constitution and the federal law. Under this doctrine, it was felt that the federal courts were the vehicle that could be utilized to combat oppression, particularly in southern states, which were operating under the guise of legalistics to keep the Negro down.

Under brilliant and dedicated leadership, the N.A.A.C.P. moved relentlessly to win many victories in the courts. The most notable of these established the right of the Negro to participate in national elections, striking down evasive devices such as the "grandfather clause," white primaries and others. Beyond doubt, the doctrine of change through legal recourse reached flood tide in the education decisions. Yet the failure of the nation, over a decade, to implement the majestic implications of these decisions caused the slow ebb of the Negro's faith in litigation as the dominant method to achieve his freedom. In his eyes, the doctrine of legal change had become the doctrine of slow token change and, as a sole weapon of struggle, now proved its unsuitability. At the time of this growing realization, during the mid-fifties, Negroes were in the grip of a crisis. Their movement no longer had a promising basic doctrine, a detailed and charted course pointing the way to their freedom.

It is an axiom of social change that no revolution can take place without a methodology suited to the circumstances of the period. During the fifties many voices offered substitutes for the tactic of legal recourse. Some called for a colossal blood bath to cleanse the nation's ills. To support their advocacy of violence and its incitement, they pointed to an historical tradition reaching back from the American Civil War to Spartacus in Rome. But the Negro in the South in 1955, assessing the power of the forces arrayed against him, could not perceive the slightest prospect of victory in this approach. He was unarmed, unorganized, untrained, disunited and, most important, psychologically and morally unprepared for the deliberate spilling of blood. Although his desperation had prepared him with the courage to die for freedom if necessary, he was not willing to commit himself to racial suicide with no prospect of victory.

Perhaps even more vital in the Negro's resistance to violence was the force of his deeply rooted spiritual beliefs. In Montgomery, after a courageous woman, Rosa Parks, had refused to move to the back of the bus, and so began the revolt that led to the boycott of 1955–56, the Negro's developing campaign against that city's racial injustice was based in the churches of the community. Throughout the South, for some years prior to Montgomery, the Negro church had emerged with increasing impact in the civil-rights struggle. Negro ministers, with a growing awareness that the true witness of a Christian life is the projection of a social gospel, had accepted leadership in the fight for racial justice, had played important roles in a number of N.A.A.C.P. groups, and were making their influence felt throughout the freedom movement.

The doctrine they preached was a nonviolent doctrine. It was not a doctrine that made their followers yearn for revenge but one that called upon them to champion change. It was not a doctrine that asked an eye for an eye but one that summoned men to seek to open the eyes of blind prejudice. The Negro turned his back on force not only because he knew he could not win his freedom through physical force but also because he believed that through physical force he could lose his soul.

There were echoes of Marcus Garvey in another solution proffered the Negro during this period of crisis and change. The Black Muslims, convinced that an interracial society promised nothing but tragedy and frustration for the Negro, began to urge a permanent separation of the races. Unlike Garvey's prescription, the Muslims appeared to believe the separation could be achieved in this country without a long sea voyage to Africa, but their message resembled Garvey's in another respect: It won only fractional support from the

Negro community. Most of those to whom the Muslims appealed were in fact expressing resentment for the lack of militancy which had long prevailed in the freedom movement. When the Negroes' fighting spirit soared in the summer of 1963, the appeal of the Muslims declined precipitously. Today, as I travel throughout the country, I am struck by how few American Negroes (except in a handful of big-city ghettos) have even heard of the Muslim movement, much less given allegiance to its pessimistic doctrine.

Yet another tactic was offered the Negro. He was encouraged to seek unity with the millions of disadvantaged whites of the South, whose basic need for social change paralleled his own. Theoretically, this proposal held a measure of logic, for it is undeniable that great masses of southern whites exist in conditions scarcely better than those which afflict the Negro. But the rationale of this theory wilted under the heat of fact. The need for immediate change was more urgently felt and more bitterly realized by the Negro than by the exploited white. As individuals, the whites could better their situation without the barrier that society places in front of a man whose racial identification by color is inescapable. Moreover, the underprivileged southern whites saw the color that separated them from Negroes more clearly than they saw the circumstances that bound them together in mutual interest. Negroes were therefore forced to face the fact that, in the South, they must move without allies; and yet the coiled power of state force made such a prospect appear both futile and quixotic.

III

Fortunately, history does not pose problems without eventually producing solutions. The disenchanted, the disadvantaged and the disinherited seem, at times of deep crisis, to summon up some sort of genius that enables them to perceive and capture the appropriate weapons to carve out their destiny. Such was the peaceable weapon of nonviolent direct action, which materialized almost overnight to inspire the Negro, and was seized in his outstretched hands with a powerful grip.

Nonviolent action, the Negro saw, was the way to supplement—not replace—the process of change through legal recourse. It was the way to divest himself of passivity without arraying himself in vindictive force. Acting in concert with fellow Negroes to assert himself as a citizen, he would embark on a militant program to demand the rights which were his: in the streets, on the buses, in the stores, the parks and other public facilities.

The religious tradition of the Negro had shown him that the nonviolent resistance of the early Christians had constituted a moral offensive of such overriding power that it shook the Roman Empire. American history had taught him that nonviolence in the form of boycotts and protests had confounded the British monarchy and laid the basis for freeing the colonies from unjust domination. Within his own century, the nonviolent ethic of Mahatma Gandhi and his followers had muzzled the guns of the British Empire in India and freed more than three hundred and fifty million people from colonialism.

Like his predecessors, the Negro was willing to risk martyrdom in order to move and stir the social conscience of his community and the nation. Instead of submitting to surreptitious cruelty in thousands of dark jail cells and on countless shadowed street corners, he would force his oppressor to commit his brutality openly—in the light of day—with the rest of the world looking on.

Acceptance of nonviolent direct action was a proof of a certain sophistication on the part of the Negro masses; for it showed that they dared to break with the old, ingrained concepts of our society. The eye-for-an-eye philosophy, the impulse to defend oneself when attacked, has always been held as the highest measure of American manhood. We are a nation that worships the frontier tradition, and our heroes are those who champion justice through violent retaliation against injustice. It is not simple to adopt the credo that moral force has as much strength and virtue as the capacity to return a physical blow; or that to refrain from hitting back requires more will and bravery than the automatic reflexes of defense.

Yet there is something in the American ethos that responds to the strength of moral force. I am reminded of the popular and widely respected novel and film *To Kill a Mockingbird*. Atticus Finch, a white southern lawyer, confronts a group of his neighbors who have become a lynch-crazed mob, seeking the life of his Negro client. Finch, armed with nothing more lethal than a lawbook, disperses the mob with the force of his moral courage, aided by his small daughter, who, innocently calling the would-be lynchers by name, reminds them that they are individual men, not a pack of beasts.

To the Negro in 1963, as to Atticus Finch, it had become obvious that nonviolence could symbolize the gold badge of heroism rather than the white feather of cowardice. In addition to being consistent with his religious precepts, it served his need to act on his own for his own liberation. It enabled him to transmute hatred into constructive energy, to seek not only to free himself but to free his oppressor from his sins. This transformation, in turn, had the marvelous effect of changing the face of the enemy. The enemy the Negro faced became not the individual who had oppressed him but the evil system which permitted that individual to do so.

The argument that nonviolence is a coward's refuge lost its force as its heroic and often perilous acts uttered their wordless but convincing rebuttal in Montgomery, in the sit-ins, on the freedom rides, and finally in Birmingham.

There is a powerful motivation when a suppressed people enlist in an army that marches under the banner of nonviolence. A nonviolent army has a magnificent universal quality. To join an army that trains its adherents in the methods of violence, you must be of a certain age. But in Birmingham, some of the most valued foot soldiers were youngsters ranging from elementary pupils to teenage high school and college students. For acceptance in the armies that maim and kill, one must be physically sound, possessed of straight limbs and accurate vision. But in Birmingham, the lame and the halt and the crippled could and did join up. Al Hibbler, the sightless singer, would never have been accepted in the United States Army or the army of any other nation, but he held a commanding position in our ranks.

In armies of violence, there is a caste of rank. In Birmingham, outside of the few generals and lieutenants who necessarily directed and coordinated operations, the regiments of the demonstrators marched in democratic phalanx. Doctors marched with window cleaners. Lawyers demonstrated with laundresses. Ph.D.'s and no-D.'s were treated with perfect equality by the registrars of the nonviolence movement.

As the broadcasting profession will confirm, no shows are so successful as those which allow for audience participation. In order to be somebody, people must feel themselves part of something. In the nonviolent army, there is room for everyone who wants to join up. There is no color distinction. There is no examination, no pledge, except that, as a soldier in the armies of violence is expected to inspect his carbine and keep it clean, nonviolent soldiers are called upon to examine and burnish their greatest weapons—their heart, their conscience, their courage and their sense of justice.

Nonviolent resistance paralyzed and confused the power structures against which it was directed. The brutality with which officials would have quelled the black individual became impotent when it could not be pursued with stealth and remain unobserved. It was caught—as a fugitive from a penitentiary is often caught—in gigantic circling spotlights. It was imprisoned in a luminous glare revealing the naked truth to the whole world. It is true that some demonstrators suffered violence, and that a few paid the extreme penalty of death. They were the martyrs of last summer who laid down their lives to put an end to the brutalizing of thousands who had been beaten and bruised and killed in dark streets and back rooms of sheriffs' offices, day in and day out, in hundreds of summers past.

The striking thing about the nonviolent crusade of 1963 was that so few felt the sting of bullets or the clubbing of billies and nightsticks. Looking back, it becomes obvious that the oppressors were restrained not only because the world was looking but also because, standing before them, were hundreds, sometimes thousands, of Negroes who for the first time dared to look back at a white man, eye to eye. Whether through a decision to exercise wise restraint or the operation of a guilty conscience, many a hand was stayed on a police club and many a fire hose was restrained from vomiting forth its pressure. That the Revolution was a comparatively bloodless one is explained by the fact that the Negro did not merely give lip service to nonviolence. The tactics the movement utilized, and that guided far-flung actions in cities dotted across the map, discouraged violence because one side would not resort to it and the other was so often immobilized by confusion, uncertainty and disunity.

Nonviolence had tremendous psychological importance to the Negro. He had to win and to vindicate his dignity in order to merit and enjoy his self-esteem. He had to let white men know that the picture of him as a clown—irresponsible, resigned and believing in his own inferiority—was a stereotype with no validity. This method was grasped by the Negro masses because it embodied the dignity of struggle, of moral conviction and self-sacrifice. The Negro was able to face his adversary, to concede to him a physical advantage and to defeat him because the superior force of the oppressor had become powerless.

To measure what this meant to the Negro may not be easy. But I am convinced that the courage and discipline with which Negro thousands accepted nonviolence healed the internal wounds of Negro millions who did not themselves march in the streets or sit in the jails of the South. One need not participate directly in order to be involved. For Negroes all over this nation, to identify with the movement, to have pride in those who were the principals, and to give moral, financial or spiritual support were to restore to them some of the pride and honor which had been stripped from them over the centuries.

IV

In the light of last summer's successful crusade, one might ask why it took the Negro eight years to apply the lessons of the Montgomery boycott to the problems of Birmingham, and the nation's other Birminghams, north and south.

A methodology and philosophy of revolution is neither born nor accepted overnight. From the moment it emerges, it is subjected to rigorous tests, opposition, scorn and prejudice. The old guard in any society resents new methods, for old guards wear the decorations and medals won by waging battle in the accepted manner. Often opposition comes not only from the conservatives, who cling to tradition, but also from the extremist militants, who favor neither the old nor the new.

Many of these extremists misread the significance and intent of nonviolence because they failed to perceive that militancy is also the father of the nonviolent way. Angry exhortation from street corners and stirring calls for the Negro to arm and go forth to do battle stimulate loud applause. But when the applause dies, the stirred and the stirring return to their homes, and lie in their beds for still one more night with no progress in view. They cannot solve the problem they face because they have offered no challenge but only a call to arms, which they themselves are unwilling to lead, knowing that doom would be its reward. They cannot solve the problem because they seek to overcome a negative situation with negative means. They cannot solve the problem because they do not reach and move into sustained action the large groups of people necessary to attract attention and convey the determination of the majority. The conservatives who say, "Let us not move so fast," and the extremists who say, "Let us go out and whip the world," would tell you that they are as far apart as the poles. But there is a striking parallel: They accomplish nothing; for they do not reach the people who have a crying need to be free.

One factor that helps to explain why the Negro nationally did not embrace the nonviolent ethic, immediately after Montgomery, was a fallacious and dangerously divisive philosophy spread by those who were either dishonest or ignorant. This philosophy held that nonviolent, direct action was a *substitute* for all other approaches, attacking especially the legal methods that up to the mid-fifties had brought such important, decisive court rulings and laws into being. The best way to defeat an army is to divide it. Negroes as well as whites have compounded confusion and distorted reality by defending the legal approach and condemning direct action, or defending direct action and condemning the legal approach.

Direct action is not a substitute for work in the courts and the halls of government. Bringing about passage of a new and broad law by a city council, state legislature or the Congress, or pleading cases before the courts of the land, does not eliminate the necessity for bringing about the mass dramatization of injustice in front of a city hall. Indeed, direct action and legal action complement one another; when skillfully employed, each becomes more effective.

The chronology of the sit-ins confirms this observation. Spontaneously born, but guided by the theory of nonviolent resistance, the lunch-counter sit-ins accomplished integration in hundreds of communities at the swiftest rate of change in the civil-rights movement up to that time. Yet, many communities successfully resisted lunch-counter desegregation, and pressed charges against the demonstrators. It was correct and effective that demonstrators should fill the jails; but it was necessary that these foot soldiers for freedom not be deserted to languish there or to pay excessive penalties for their devotion. Indeed, by creative use of the law, it was possible to prove that officials combating the demonstrations were using the power of the police state to deny the Negro equal protection under the law. This brought many of the cases squarely under the jurisdiction of the Fourteenth Amendment. As a consequence of combining direct and legal action, far-reaching precedents were established, which served, in turn, to extend the areas of desegregation.

Another reason for the delay in applying the lessons of Montgomery was the feeling abroad in the land that the success of the bus boycott was an isolated phenomenon, and that the Negro elsewhere would never be willing to sacrifice in such extreme measure. When, in Albany, Georgia, in 1962, months of demonstrations and jailings failed to accomplish the goals of the movement, reports in the press and elsewhere pronounced nonviolent resistance a dead issue.

There were weaknesses in Albany, and a share of the responsibility belongs to each of us who participated. However, none of us was so immodest as to feel himself master of the new theory. Each of us expected that setbacks would be a part of the ongoing effort. There is no tactical theory so neat that a revolutionary struggle for a share of power can be won merely by pressing a row of buttons. Human beings with all their faults and strengths constitute the mechanism of a social movement. They must make mistakes and learn from them, make more mistakes and learn anew. They must taste defeat as well as success, and discover how to live with each. Time and action are the teachers.

When we planned our strategy for Birmingham months later, we spent many hours assessing Albany and trying to learn from its errors. Our appraisals not only helped to make our subsequent tactics more effective, but revealed that Albany was far from an unqualified failure. Though lunch counters remained segregated, thousands of Negroes were added to the voting-registration rolls. In the gubernatorial elections that followed our summer there, a moderate candidate confronted a rabid segregationist. By reason of the expanded Negro vote, the moderate defeated the segregationist in the city of Albany, which in turn contributed to his victory in the state. As a result, Georgia elected its first governor pledged to respect and enforce the law equally.

Our movement had been checked in Albany but not defeated. City authorities had been obliged to close down facilities such as parks, libraries and bus lines to avoid integration. The authorities were crippling themselves, denying facilities to the white population in order to obstruct our progress. Someone observed that Samuel Johnson had called parks "the lungs of a city," and that Albany would have to breathe again even though the air, too, be desegregated.

Even had nonviolent resistance been soundly defeated in Albany, the alacrity with which the bells were tolled for it must arouse suspicion. The prompt interment of the theory was not a judicious conclusion but an attack. Albany, in fact, had proved how extraordinary was the Negro response to the appeal of nonviolence. Approximately 5 percent of the total Negro population went willingly to jail. Were that percentage duplicated in New York City, some fifty thousand Negroes would overflow its prisons. If a people can produce from its ranks 5 percent who will go voluntarily to jail for a just cause, surely nothing can thwart its ultimate triumph.

If, however, the detractors of nonviolence fell into error by magnifying temporary setbacks into catastrophic defeat, the adherents of the new theory must avoid exaggerating its powers. When we speak of filling the jails, we are talking of a tactic to be flexibly applied. No responsible person would promise to fill all jails everywhere at any time. Leaders indulge in bombast if they do not take all circumstances into account before calling upon their people to make a maximum sacrifice. Filling jails means that thousands of people must leave their jobs, perhaps to lose them, put off responsibilities, undergo harrowing psychological experiences for which law-abiding people are not routinely prepared. The miracle of nonviolence lies in the degree to which people will sacrifice under its inspiration, when the call is based on judgment.

Negroes are human, not superhuman. Like all people, they have differing personalities, diverse financial interests and varied aspirations. There are Negroes who will never fight for freedom. There are Negroes who will seek profit for themselves alone from the struggle. There are even some Negroes who will cooperate with their oppressors. These facts should distress no one. Every minority and every people has its share of opportunists, profiteers, freeloaders and escapists. The hammer blows of discrimination, poverty and segregation must warp and corrupt some. No one can pretend that because a people may be oppressed, every individual member is virtuous and worthy. The real issue is whether in the great mass the dominant characteristics are decency, honor and courage.

In 1963, once again life was proof that Negroes had their heroes, their masses of decent people, along with their lost souls. The doubts that millions had felt as to the efficacy of the nonviolent way were dissolved. And the Negro saw that by proving the sweeping and majestic power of nonviolence to bring about the beloved community, it might be possible for him to set an example to a whole world caught up in conflict.

V

In the entire country there was no place to compare with Birmingham. The largest industrial city in the South, Birmingham had become, in the thirties, a symbol for bloodshed when trade unions sought to organize. It was a community in which human rights had been trampled for so long that fear and oppression were as thick in its atmosphere as the smog from its factories. Its financial interests were interlocked with a power structure which spread throughout the South and radiated into the North.

The challenge to nonviolent, direct action could not have been staged in a more appropriate arena. In the summer of 1963, an army brandishing only the healing sword of nonviolence humbled the most powerful, the most experienced and the most implacable segregationists in the country. Birmingham was to emerge with a delicately poised peace, but without awaiting its implementation the Negro seized the weapon that had won that dangerous peace and swept across the land with it.

The victory of the theory of nonviolent direct action was a fact. Faith in this method had come to maturity in Birmingham. As a result, the whole spectrum of the civil-rights struggle would undergo basic change. Nonviolence had passed the test of its steel in the fires of turmoil. The united power of southern segregation was the hammer. Birmingham was the anvil.

III

Bull Connor's Birmingham

If you had visited Birmingham before the third of April in the one-hundredth-anniversary year of the Negro's emancipation, you might have come to a startling conclusion. You might have concluded that here was a city which had been trapped for decades in a Rip Van Winkle slumber; a city whose fathers had apparently never heard of Abraham Lincoln, Thomas Jefferson, the Bill of Rights, the Preamble to the Constitution, the Thirteenth, Fourteenth and Fifteenth Amendments, or the 1954 decision of the United States Supreme Court outlawing segregation in the public schools.

If your powers of imagination were great enough to enable you to place yourself in the position of a Negro baby born and brought up to physical maturity in Birmingham, you would have pictured your life in the following manner:

You would be born in a jim-crow hospital to parents who probably lived in a ghetto. You would attend a jim-crow school. It is not really true that the city fathers had never heard of the Supreme Court's school-desegregation order. They had heard of it and, since its passage, had consistently expressed their defiance, typified by the prediction of one official that blood would run in the streets before desegregation would be permitted to come to Birmingham.

You would spend your childhood playing mainly in the streets because the "colored" parks were abysmally inadequate. When a federal court order banned park segregation, you would find that Birmingham closed down its parks and gave up its baseball team rather than integrate them.

If you went shopping with your mother or father, you would trudge along as they purchased at every counter, except one, in the large or small stores. If you were hungry or thirsty you would have to forget about it until you got back to the Negro section of town, for in your city it was a violation of the law to serve food to Negroes at the same counter with whites.

If your family attended church, you would go to a Negro church. If you wanted to visit a church attended by white people, you would not be welcome. For although your white fellow citizens would insist that they were Christians, they practiced segregation as rigidly in the house of God as they did in the theater.

If you loved music and yearned to hear the Metropolitan Opera on its tour of the South, you could not enjoy this privilege. Nor could your white fellow music-lovers; for the Metropolitan had discontinued scheduling Birmingham on its national tours after it had adopted a policy of not performing before segregated audiences.

If you wanted to contribute to and be a part of the work of the National Association for the Advancement of Colored People, you would not be able to join a local branch. In the state of Alabama, segregationist authorities had been successful in enjoining the N.A.A.C.P. from performing its civil-rights work by declaring it a "foreign corporation" and rendering its activities illegal.

If you wanted a job in this city—one of the greatest iron- and steel-producing centers in the nation—you had better settle on doing menial work as a porter or laborer. If you were fortunate enough to get a job, you could expect that promotions to a better status or more pay would come, not to you, but to a white employee regardless of your comparative talents. On your job, you would eat in a separate place and use a water fountain and lavatory labeled "Colored" in conformity to citywide ordinances.

If you believed your history books and thought of America as a country whose governing officials—whether city, state or nation—are selected by the governed, you would be swiftly disillusioned when you tried to exercise your right to register and vote. You would be confronted with every conceivable obstacle to taking that most important walk a Negro American can take today—the walk to the ballot box. Of the 80,000 voters in Birmingham, prior to January 1963, only 10,000 were Negroes. Your race, constituting two-fifths of the city's population, would make up one-eighth of its voting strength.

You would be living in a city where brutality directed against Negroes was an unquestioned and unchallenged reality. One of the city commissioners, a member of the body that ruled municipal affairs, would be Eugene "Bull" Connor, a racist who prided himself on knowing how to handle the Negro and keep him in his "place." As Commissioner of Public Safety, Bull Connor, entrenched for many years in a key position in the Birmingham power structure, displayed as much contempt for the rights of the Negro as he did defiance for the authority of the federal government.

You would have found a general atmosphere of violence and brutality in Birmingham. Local racists have intimidated, mobbed, and even killed Negroes with impunity. One of the more vivid and recent examples of the terror of Birmingham was the castration of a Negro man, whose mutilated body had then been abandoned on a lonely road. No Negro home was protected from bombings and burnings. From the year 1957 through January of 1963, while Birmingham was still claiming that its Negroes were "satisfied," seventeen unsolved bombings of Negro churches and homes of civil-rights leaders had occurred.

Negroes were not the only persons who suffered because of Bull Connor's rule. It was Birmingham's Safety Commissioner who, in 1961, arrested the manager of the local bus station when the latter sought to obey the law of the land by serving Negroes. Although a federal district judge condemned Connor in strong terms for this action and released the victim, the fact remained that in Birmingham, early in 1963, no places of public accommodation were integrated except the bus station, the train station and the airport.

In Bull Connor's Birmingham, you would be a resident of a city where a United States senator, visiting to deliver a speech, had been arrested because he walked through a door marked "Colored."

In Connor's Birmingham, the silent password was fear. It was a fear not only on the part of the black oppressed, but also in the hearts of the white oppressors. Guilt was a part of their fear. There was also the dread of change, that all too prevalent fear which hounds those whose attitudes have been hardened by the long winter of reaction. Many were apprehensive of social ostracism. Certainly Birmingham had its white moderates who disapproved of Bull Connor's tactics. Certainly Birmingham had its decent white citizens who privately deplored the maltreatment of Negroes. But they remained publicly silent. It was a silence born of fear—fear of social, political and economic reprisals. The ultimate tragedy of Birmingham was not the brutality of the bad people, but the silence of the good people.

In Birmingham, you would be living in a community where the white man's long-lived tyranny had cowed your people, led them to abandon hope, and developed in them a false sense of inferiority. You would be living in a city where the representatives of economic and political power refused to even discuss social justice with the leaders of your people.

You would be living in the largest city of a police state, presided over by a governor—George Wallace—whose inauguration vow had been a pledge of "segregation now, segregation tomorrow, segregation forever!" You would be living, in fact, in the most segregated city in America.

II

There was one threat to the reign of white supremacy in Birmingham. As an outgrowth of the Montgomery bus boycott, protest movements had sprung up in numerous cities across the South. In Birmingham, one of the nation's most courageous freedom fighters, the Reverend Fred Shuttlesworth, had organized the Alabama Christian Movement for Human Rights—A.C.H.R.—in the spring of 1956. Shuttlesworth, a wiry, energetic and indomitable man, had set out to change Birmingham and to end for all time the terrorist, racist rule of Bull Connor.

When Shuttlesworth first formed his organization—which soon became one of the eighty-five affiliates of our Southern Christian Leadership Conference—Bull Connor doubtless regarded the group as just another bunch of troublesome "niggers." It soon became obvious even to Connor, however, that Shuttlesworth was in dead earnest. A.C.H.R. grew, month by month, to become the acknowledged basic mass movement of the Birmingham Negro. Weekly mass meetings were held at various churches. The meetings were packed. A.C.H.R. began working through the courts to compel the city to relax its segregation policies. A suit was instituted to open Birmingham's public-recreation facilities to all of its citizens. It was when the city lost this case that the authorities responded by closing down the parks, rather than permit Negro youngsters to share facilities maintained by the taxes of black and white alike.

Early in 1962, students at Miles College initiated a

staggered series of boycotts against downtown white merchants. Shuttlesworth and his fellow leaders of A.C.H.R. joined with the students and helped them to mobilize many of Birmingham's Negroes in a determined withdrawal of business from stores that displayed jim-crow signs, refused to hire Negroes in other than menial capacities, refused to promote the few Negroes in their employ, and would not serve colored people at their lunch counters. As a result of the campaign, business fell off as much as 40 percent at some downtown stores. Fred was leading a militant crusade, but Birmingham and Bull Connor fought, tooth and nail, to keep things as they were.

As the parent organization of A.C.H.R., the Southern Christian Leadership Conference in Atlanta had kept a close and admiring watch on Fred Shuttlesworth's uphill fight. We knew that he had paid the price in personal suffering for the battle he was waging. He had been jailed several times. His home and church had been badly damaged by bombs. Yet he had refused to back down. This courageous minister's audacious public defiance of Bull Connor had become a source of inspiration and encouragement to Negroes throughout the South.

In the May 1962 board meeting of S.C.L.C. at Chattanooga, we decided to give serious consideration to joining Shuttlesworth and A.C.H.R. in a massive direct-action campaign to attack segregation in Birmingham. It happened that we had scheduled that city as the site of our forthcoming annual convention in September. Immediately after the board meeting, rumors began to circulate in Birmingham that S.C.L.C.

had definitely decided to support Fred's fight by mounting a prolonged campaign in that city at the time of the convention. These rumors gained so much impetus that stories supporting them appeared in the daily press. For the first time, Birmingham businessmen, who had pursued a policy of ignoring demands for integration, became concerned and concluded that they would have to do something drastic to forestall large-scale protest.

Several weeks before our convention was scheduled, the business community began negotiating with A.C.H.R. Meeting with the white Senior Citizens Committee were Shuttlesworth; Dr. Lucius Pitts, president of Miles College; A. G. Gaston, wealthy businessman and owner of the Gaston Motel; Arthur Shores, an attorney with wide experience in civil-rights cases; the Reverend Edward Gardner, vice president of A.C.H.R.; and insurance broker John Drew. After several talks, the group came to some basic agreements. As a first step, some of the merchants agreed to remove the jim-crow signs from their stores, and several actually did so. The businessmen further agreed to join in a suit with A.C.H.R. to seek nullification of city ordinances forbidding integration at lunch counters. It appeared that a small crack had opened in Birmingham.

Although wary of the permanence of these promises, the Negro group decided to give the merchants a chance to demonstrate their good faith. Shuttlesworth called a press conference to announce that a moratorium had been declared on boycotts and demonstrations. However, to protect the position of A.C.H.R., he made it clear that his organization's parent body, S.C.L.C., would be coming to Birmingham for its convention as planned, and informed the press that after the convention, S.C.L.C. would be asked to return to the Steel City to help launch an action campaign if the pledges of the business community were violated.

Bull Connor had been issuing ominous statements about our forthcoming meeting. When he realized that his threats were frightening no one, he began to try to intimidate the press by announcing that the press cards of any "outside reporters" would be taken away from them. It was clear that Connor felt the bastions of segregation could be most securely maintained in Birmingham if national exposure could be avoided.

The S.C.L.C. convention took place in September 1962, as scheduled. Shortly thereafter, Fred Shuttlesworth's fears were justified: The jim-crow signs reappeared in the stores. The rumor was that Bull Connor had threatened some of the merchants with loss of their licenses if they did not restore the signs. It seemed obvious to Fred that the merchants had never intended to keep any of their promises; their token action had merely been calculated to stall off demonstrations while S.C.L.C. was in the city. During a series of lengthy telephone calls between Birmingham and Atlanta, we reached the conclusion that we had no alternative but to go through with our proposed combined-action campaign.

III

Along with Fred Shuttlesworth, we believed that while a campaign in Birmingham would surely be the toughest fight of our civil-rights careers, it could, if successful, break the back of segregation all over the nation.

This city had been the country's chief symbol of racial intolerance. A victory there might well set forces in motion to change the entire course of the drive for freedom and justice. Because we were convinced of the significance of the job to be done in Birmingham, we decided that the most thorough planning and prayerful preparation must go into the effort. We began to prepare a top-secret file which we called "Project C"— the "C" for Birmingham's *Confrontation* with the fight for justice and morality in race relations.

In preparation for our campaign, I called a three-day retreat and planning session with S.C.L.C. staff and board members at our training center near Savannah, Georgia. Here we sought to perfect a timetable and discuss every possible eventuality. In analyzing our campaign in Albany, Georgia, we decided that one of the principal mistakes we had made there was to scatter our efforts too widely. We had been so involved in attacking segregation in general that we had failed to direct our protest effectively to any one major facet. We concluded that in hard-core communities a more effective battle could be waged if it was concentrated against one aspect of the evil and intricate system of segregation. We decided, therefore, to center the Birmingham struggle on the business community, for we knew that the Negro population had sufficient buying power so that its withdrawal could make the difference between profit and loss for many businesses. Stores with lunch counters were our first target. There is a special humiliation for the Negro in having his money accepted at every department in a store except the lunch counter. Food is not only a necessity but a symbol, and our lunch counter campaign had not only a practical but a symbolic importance.

Two weeks after the retreat at our training center, I went to Birmingham with my able executive assistant, the Reverend Wyatt Tee Walker, and my abiding friend and fellow campaigner from the days of Montgomery, the Reverend Ralph Abernathy, S.C.L.C.'s treasurer. There we began to meet with the board of A.C.H.R. to assist in preparing the Negro community for what would surely be a difficult, prolonged and dangerous campaign.

We met in the now famous Room 30 of the Gaston Motel, situated on Fifth Avenue North, in the Negro ghetto. This room, which housed Ralph and myself, and served as the headquarters for all of the strategy sessions in subsequent months, would later be the target of one of the bombs on the fateful and violent Saturday night of May 11, the eve of Mother's Day.

The first major decision we faced was setting the date for the launching of "Project C." Since it was our aim to bring pressure to bear on the merchants, we felt that our campaign should be mounted around the Easter season—the second biggest shopping period of the year. If we started the first week of March, we would have six weeks to mobilize the community before Easter, which fell on April 14. But at this point we were reminded that a mayoralty election was to be held in Birmingham on March 5.

The leading candidates were Albert Boutwell, Eugene "Bull" Connor and Tom King. All were segregationists, running on a platform to preserve the status quo. Yet both King and Boutwell were considered moderates in comparison to Connor. We were hopeful that Connor would be so thoroughly defeated that at least we would not have to deal with him. Since we did not want our campaign to be used as a political football, we decided to postpone it, planning to begin demonstrations two weeks after the election.

Meanwhile Wyatt Walker was detailed to return to Birmingham and begin work on the mechanics of the campaign. From then on, he visited Birmingham periodically, unannounced, organizing a transportation corps and laying the groundwork for an intensive boycott. He conferred with lawyers about the city code on picketing, demonstrations and so forth, gathered data on the probable bail-bond situation, and prepared for the injunction that was certain to come.

In addition to scheduling workshops on nonviolence and direct-action techniques for our recruits, Wyatt familiarized himself with downtown Birmingham, not only plotting the main streets and landmarks (target stores, city hall, post office, etc.), but meticulously surveying each store's eating facilities, and sketching the entrances and possible paths of ingress and egress. In fact, Walker detailed the number of stools, tables and chairs to determine how many demonstrators should go to each store. His survey of the downtown area also included suggested secondary targets in the event we were blocked from reaching our primary targets. By March 1, the project was in high gear and the loose ends of organizational structure were being pulled together. Some 250 people had volunteered to participate in the initial demonstrations and had pledged to remain in jail at least five days.

At this point the results of the March 5 election intervened to pose a serious new problem. No candidate had won a clear victory. There would have to be a run-off vote, to be held the first week in April. We had hoped that if a run-off resulted, it would have been between Boutwell and King. As it turned out, the competing candidates were to be Boutwell and Connor.

Again we had to remap strategy. Had we moved in while Connor and Boutwell were electioneering, Connor would undoubtedly have capitalized on our presence by using it as an emotion-charged issue for his own political advantage, waging a vigorous campaign to persuade the white community that he, and he alone, could defend the city's official policies of segregation. We might actually have had the effect of helping Connor win. Reluctantly, we decided to postpone the demonstrations until the day after the run-off. We would have to move promptly if we were still to have time to affect Easter shopping.

We left Birmingham sadly, realizing that after this second delay the intensive groundwork we had done in the Negro community might not bring the effective results we sought. We were leaving some 250 volunteers who had been willing to join our ranks and to go to jail. Now we must lose contact with these recruits for several weeks. Yet we dared not remain. It was agreed that no member of the S.C.L.C. staff would return to Birmingham until after the run-off.

In the interim, I was busy on another preparatory measure. Realizing the difficulties that lay ahead, we felt it was vital to get the support of key people across the nation. We addressed confidential letters to the

National Association for the Advancement of Colored
People, the Congress of Racial Equality, the Student
Nonviolent Coordinating Committee and the Southern Regional Council, telling them of our plans and
advising them that we might be calling on them for aid.
We corresponded in the same vein with the seventy-
five religious leaders of all faiths who had joined us in
the Albany Movement.

In New York City, Harry Belafonte, an old friend
and supporter of S.C.L.C, agreed to call a meeting at
his apartment. Approximately seventy-five New York-
ers were present. They were a cross section of citizens,
including newspapermen (who kept their promise not
to publish stories about the meeting until the action
was launched), clergymen, business and professional
people, and unofficial representatives from the offices
of Mayor Wagner and Governor Rockefeller.

Fred Shuttlesworth and I spoke of the problems then
existing in Birmingham and those we anticipated. We
explained why we had delayed taking action until after
the run-off, and why we felt it necessary to proceed
with our plans whether Connor or Boutwell was the
eventual victor. Shuttlesworth, wearing the scars of
earlier battles, brought a sense of the danger as well as
the earnestness of our crusade into that peaceful New
York living room. Although many of those present had
worked with S.C.L.C. in the past, there was a silence
almost like the shock of a fresh discovery when Shuttlesworth said, "You have to be prepared to die before
you can begin to live."

When we had finished, the most frequent question
was: "What can we do to help?"

We answered that we were certain to need tremendous sums of money for bail bonds. We might need public meetings to organize more support. On the spot, Harry Belafonte organized a committee, and money was pledged the same night. For the next three weeks, Belafonte, who never does anything without being totally involved, gave unlimited hours to organizing people and money. Throughout the subsequent campaign, he talked with me or my aides two or three times a day. It would be hard to overestimate the role this sensitive artist played in the success of the Birmingham crusade.

Similar meetings were held with two of our strongest affiliates, the Western Christian Leadership Conference in Los Angeles, and the Virginia Christian Leadership Conference in Richmond. Both pledged and gave their unswerving support to the campaign. Later on, with the N.A.A.C.P. and other local organizations, the Western Conference raised the largest amount of money—some $75,000—which has ever been raised in a single rally for S.C.L.C. Many of the men from these conferences would later join our ranks during the crisis.

With these contacts established, the time had come to return to Birmingham. The run-off election was April 2. We flew in the same night. By word of mouth, we set about trying to make contact with our 250 volunteers for an unadvertised meeting. About sixty-five came out. The following day, with this modest task force, we launched the direct-action campaign in Birmingham.

IV

New Day in Birmingham

On Wednesday, April 3, 1963, the Birmingham *News* appeared on the stands, its front page bright with a color drawing showing a golden sun rising over the city. It was captioned: "New Day Dawns for Birmingham," and celebrated Albert Boutwell's victory in the run-off vote for mayor. The golden glow of racial harmony, the headline implied, could now be expected to descend on the city. As events were to show, it was indeed a new day for Birmingham; but not because Boutwell had won the election.

For all the optimism expressed in the press and elsewhere, we were convinced that Albert Boutwell was, in Fred Shuttlesworth's apt phrase, "just a dignified Bull Connor." We knew that the former state senator and lieutenant governor had been the principal author of Alabama's Pupil Placement Law, and was a consistent supporter of segregationist views. His statement a few days after election that "we citizens of Birmingham respect and understand one another" showed that he understood nothing about two-fifths of Birmingham's citizens, to whom even polite segregation was no respect.

Meanwhile, despite the results of the run-off, the city commissioners, including Bull Connor, had taken the position that they could not legally be removed from office until 1965. They would go into the courts to defend their position, and refused in the interim to move out of their City Hall offices. If they won in court (and conflict in the laws of Birmingham made this theoretically possible), they would remain in office for another two years. If they lost, their terms would still not expire until April 15, the day after Easter. In either case, we were committed to enter the situation in a city which was operating literally under two governments.

We had decided to limit the first few days' efforts to sit-ins. Being prepared for a long struggle, we felt it best to begin modestly, with a limited number of arrests each day. By rationing our energies in this manner, we would help toward the buildup and drama of a growing campaign. The first demonstrations were, accordingly, not spectacular, but they were well organized. Operating on a precise timetable, small groups maintained a series of sit-ins at lunch counters in the downtown department stores and drugstores. When the demonstrators were asked to leave and refused, they were arrested under the local "trespass after warning" ordinance. By Friday night, there had been no disturbances worth note. Evidently neither Bull Connor nor the merchants expected this quiet beginning to blossom into a large-scale operation.

After the first day we held a mass meeting, the first of sixty-five nightly meetings conducted at various churches in the Negro community. Through these meetings we were able to generate the power and depth which finally galvanized the entire Negro community. The mass meetings had a definite pattern, shaped by some of the finest activists in the civil-rights movement. Ralph Abernathy, with his unique combination of humor and dedication, has a genius for lifting an audience to heights of enthusiasm and holding it there. When he plants himself behind the lectern, squat and powerful, his round face breaking easily into laughter, his listeners both love and believe him. Wyatt Walker, youthful, lean and bespectacled, brought his energetic and untiring spirit to our meetings, whose members already knew and admired his dedicated work as a behind-the-scenes organizer of the campaign. There was a special adulation that went out to the fiery words and determined zeal of Fred Shuttlesworth, who had proved to his people that he would not ask anyone to go where he was not willing to lead. Although for the first week I was busy on matters that prevented my taking an active part in the demonstrations, I spoke at the mass meetings nightly on the philosophy of nonviolence and its methods. Besides these "regulars," local speakers appeared from time to time to describe the injustices and humiliation of being a Negro in Birmingham, and occasional visitors from elsewhere across the country brought us welcome messages of support.

An important part of the mass meetings was the freedom songs. In a sense the freedom songs are the soul of the movement. They are more than just incantations of clever phrases designed to invigorate a campaign; they are as old as the history of the Negro in America.

They are adaptations of the songs the slaves sang—the sorrow songs, the shouts for joy, the battle hymns and the anthems of our movement. I have heard people talk of their beat and rhythm, but we in the movement are as inspired by their words. "Woke Up This Morning with My Mind Stayed on Freedom" is a sentence that needs no music to make its point. We sing the freedom songs today for the same reason the slaves sang them, because we too are in bondage and the songs add hope to our determination that "We shall overcome, Black and white together, We shall overcome someday."

I have stood in a meeting with hundreds of youngsters and joined in while they sang "Ain't Gonna Let Nobody Turn Me 'Round." It is not just a song; it is a resolve. A few minutes later, I have seen those same youngsters refuse to turn around from the onrush of a police dog, refuse to turn around before a pugnacious Bull Connor in command of men armed with power hoses. These songs bind us together, give us courage together, help us to march together.

Toward the end of the mass meetings, Abernathy or Shuttlesworth or I would extend an appeal for volunteers to serve in our nonviolent army. We made it clear that we would not send anyone out to demonstrate who had not convinced himself and us that he could accept and endure violence without retaliating. At the same time, we urged the volunteers to give up any possible weapons that they might have on their persons. Hundreds of people responded to this appeal. Some of those who carried penknives, Boy Scout knives—all kinds of knives—had them not because they wanted to use them against the police or other attackers, but because they wanted to defend themselves against Mr. Connor's dogs. We proved to them that we needed no weapons —not so much as a toothpick. We proved that we possessed the most formidable weapon of all—the conviction that we were right. We had the protection of our knowledge that we were more concerned about realizing our righteous aims than about saving our skins.

The invitational periods at the mass meetings, when we asked for volunteers, were much like those invitational periods that occur every Sunday morning in Negro churches, when the pastor projects the call to those present to join the church. By twenties and thirties and forties, people came forward to join our army. We did not hesitate to call our movement an army. But it was a special army, with no supplies but its sincerity, no uniform but its determination, no arsenal except its faith, no currency but its conscience. It was an army that would move but not maul. It was an army that would sing but not slay. It was an army that would flank but not falter. It was an army to storm bastions of hatred, to lay siege to the fortresses of segregation, to surround symbols of discrimination. It was an army whose allegiance was to God and whose strategy and intelligence were the eloquently simple dictates of conscience.

As the meetings continued and as the battle for the soul of Birmingham quickened and caught the attention of the world, the meetings were more crowded and the volunteers more numerous. Men, women and children came forward to shake hands, and then proceeded to the back of the church, where the Leadership

Training Committee made an appointment with them to come to our office the following day for screening and intensive training.

The focus of these training sessions was the socio-dramas designed to prepare the demonstrators for some of the challenges they could expect to face. The harsh language and physical abuse of the police and the self-appointed guardians of the law were frankly presented, along with the nonviolent creed in action: to resist without bitterness; to be cursed and not reply; to be beaten and not hit back. The S.C.L.C. staff members who conducted these sessions played their roles with the conviction born of experience. They included the Reverend James Lawson, expelled from Vanderbilt University a few years back for his militant civil-rights work, and one of the country's leading exponents of the nonviolent credo; the Reverend James Bevel, already an experienced leader in Nashville, Greenwood and other campaigns; his wife, Diane Nash Bevel, who as a student at Fisk had become an early symbol of the young Negroes' thrust toward freedom; the Reverend Bernard Lee, whose devotion to civil rights dated back to his leadership of the student movement at Alabama State College; the Reverend Andy Young, our able and dedicated program director; and Dorothy Cotton, director of our ongoing Citizenship Education Program, who also brought her rich talent for song to the heart of the movement.

Not all who volunteered could pass our strict tests for service as demonstrators. But there was much to be done, over and above the dramatic act of presenting one's body in the marches. There were errands to be run, phone calls to be made, typing, so many things. If a volunteer wasn't suited to march, he was utilized in one of a dozen other ways to help the cause. Every volunteer was required to sign a Commitment Card that read:

I HEREBY PLEDGE MYSELF—MY PERSON AND BODY—TO THE NONVIOLENT MOVEMENT. THEREFORE I WILL KEEP THE FOLLOWING TEN COMMANDMENTS:

1. MEDITATE daily on the teachings and life of Jesus.
2. REMEMBER always that the nonviolent movement in Birmingham seeks justice and reconciliation— not victory.
3. WALK and TALK in the manner of love, for God is love.
4. PRAY daily to be used by God in order that all men might be free.
5. SACRIFICE personal wishes in order that all men might be free.
6. OBSERVE with both friend and foe the ordinary rules of courtesy.
7. SEEK to perform regular service for others and for the world.
8. REFRAIN from the violence of fist, tongue, or heart.
9. STRIVE to be in good spiritual and bodily health.
10. FOLLOW the directions of the movement and of the captain on a demonstration.

I sign this pledge, having seriously considered what I do and with the determination and will to persevere.

Name _____

Address _____

Phone _____

Nearest Relative _____

Address _____

Besides demonstrations, I could also help the movement by: (Circle the proper items)

Run errands, Drive my car, Fix food for volunteers, Clerical work, Make phone calls, Answer phones, Mimeograph, Type, Print signs, Distribute leaflets.

ALABAMA CHRISTIAN MOVEMENT
FOR HUMAN RIGHTS
Birmingham Affiliate of S.C.L.C.
505½ North 17th Street
F. L. Shuttlesworth, President

II

I had planned to submit myself to imprisonment two or three days after our demonstrations began. It didn't take long after returning to Birmingham, however, to recognize the existence of a problem that made it unwise and impractical for me to go to jail before something had been done to solve it.

We had been forced to change our timetable twice.

We had had to make a strategic retreat until after the run-off and had lost contact with the community for several weeks. We had returned now to a city whose political power structure was divided. We had returned to find that our own people were not united. There was tremendous resistance to our program from some of the Negro ministers, businessmen and professionals in the city. This opposition did not exist because these Negroes did not want to be free. It existed for several other reasons.

The Negro in Birmingham, like the Negro elsewhere in this nation, had been skillfully brainwashed to the point where he had accepted the white man's theory that he, as a Negro, was inferior. He wanted to believe that he was the equal of any man; but he didn't know where to begin or how to resist the influences that had conditioned him to take the line of least resistance and go along with the white man's views. He knew that there were exceptions to the white man's evaluation: a Ralph Bunche, a Jackie Robinson, a Marian Anderson. But to the Negro, in Birmingham and in the nation, the exception did not prove the rule.

Another consideration had also affected the thinking of some of the Negro leaders in Birmingham. This was the widespread feeling that our action was ill-timed, and that we should have given the new Boutwell government a chance. Attorney General Robert Kennedy had been one of the first to voice this criticism. The *Washington Post,* which covered Birmingham from the first day of our demonstrations, had editorially attacked our "timing." In fact, virtually all the coverage in the national press at first had been negative, picturing us as irresponsible hotheads who had plunged into a situation just when Birmingham was getting ready to change overnight into Paradise. The sudden emergence of our protest seemed to give the lie to this vision.

In Montgomery, during the bus boycott, and in the Albany, Georgia, campaign, we had had the advantage of a sympathetic and understanding national press from the outset. In Birmingham we did not. It is terribly difficult to wage such a battle without the moral support of the national press to counteract the hostility of local editors. The words "bad timing" came to be ghosts haunting our every move in Birmingham. Yet people who used this argument were ignorant of the background of our planning. They did not know we had postponed our campaign twice. They did not know our reason for attacking in time to affect Easter shopping. Above all they did not realize that it was ridiculous to speak of timing when the clock of history showed that the Negro had already suffered one hundred years of delay.

Not only were many of the Negro leaders affected by the administration's position, but they were themselves indulging in a false optimism about what would happen to Birmingham under the new government. The situation had been critical for so many years that, I suppose, these people felt that any change represented a giant step toward the good. Many truly believed that once the influence of Bull Connor had faded, everything was going to be all right.

Another reason for the opposition within the Negro community was resentment on the part of some groups and leaders because we had not kept them informed about the date we planned to begin or the strategy we would adopt. They felt that they were being pulled in on something they had no part in organizing. They did not realize that, because of the local political situation, we had been forced to keep our plans secret.

We were seeking to bring about a great social change which could only be achieved through unified effort. Yet our community was divided. Our goals could never be attained in such an atmosphere. It was decided that we would conduct a whirlwind campaign of meetings with organizations and leaders in the Negro community, to seek to mobilize every key person and group behind our movement.

Along with members of my staff, I began addressing numerous groups representing a cross section of our people in Birmingham. I spoke to 125 business and professional people at a call meeting in the Gaston Building. I talked to a gathering of two hundred ministers. I met with many smaller groups, during a hectic one-week schedule. In most cases, the atmosphere when I entered was tense and chilly, and I was aware that there was a great deal of work to be done.

I went immediately to the point, explaining to the business and professional men why we had been forced to proceed without letting them know the date in advance. I dealt with the argument of timing. To the ministers I stressed the need for a social gospel to supplement the gospel of individual salvation. I suggested that only a "dry as dust" religion prompts a minister to extol the glories of heaven while ignoring the social conditions that cause men an earthly hell. I pleaded for the projection of strong, firm leadership by the Negro minister, pointing out that he is freer, more independent, than any other person in the community. I asked how the Negro would ever gain his freedom without the guidance, support and inspiration of his spiritual leaders.

I challenged those who had been persuaded that I was an "outsider." I pointed out that Fred Shuttlesworth's Alabama Christian Movement for Human Rights was an affiliate of the Southern Christian Leadership Conference, and that the Shuttlesworth group had asked S.C.L.C. to come to Birmingham, and that as president of S.C.L.C., I had come in the interests of aiding an S.C.L.C. affiliate.

I expanded further on the weary and worn "outsider" charge, which we have faced in every community where we have gone to try to help. No Negro, in fact, no American, is an outsider when he goes to any community to aid the cause of freedom and justice. No Negro anywhere, regardless of his social standing, his financial status, his prestige and position, is an outsider so long as dignity and decency are denied to the humblest black child in Mississippi, Alabama or Georgia.

The amazing aftermath of Birmingham, the sweeping Negro Revolution, revealed to people all over the land that there are no outsiders in all these fifty states of America. When a police dog buried his fangs in the ankle of a small child in Birmingham, he buried his fangs in the ankle of every American. The bell of man's inhumanity to man does not toll for any one man. It tolls for you, for me, for all of us.

Somehow God gave me the power to transform the resentments, the suspicions, the fears and the misunderstanding I found that week into faith and enthusiasm. I spoke from my heart, and out of each meeting came firm endorsements and pledges of participation and support. With the new unity that developed and now poured fresh blood into our protest, the foundations of the old order were doomed. A new order was destined to be born, and not all the powers of bigotry or Bull Connor could abort it.

III

By the end of the first three days of lunch-counter sit-ins, there had been thirty-five arrests. On Saturday, April 6, we began the next stage of our crusade with a march on City Hall. Carefully selected and screened, the first waves of demonstrators conducted themselves exactly as they had been trained to do. They marched in orderly files of two, without banners or band or singing. When they reached a point, three blocks from their goal, where Bull Connor's officers loomed in their path, they stood silently by as their leaders politely but firmly refused to obey Connor's orders to disperse. Thereupon forty-two were arrested for "parading without a permit." They were escorted with amazing politeness into the paddy wagons, and they, in turn, allowed themselves to be led without resisting, singing freedom songs on the way to jail. The sidewalks were lined with cheering Negroes, singing and lustily applauding their jailbound heroes—for this is exactly what they were in the eyes of their neighbors and friends. Something was happening to the Negro in this city, just as something revolutionary was taking place in the mind, heart and soul of Negroes all over America.

From then on, the daily demonstrations grew stronger. Our boycott of the downtown merchants was proving amazingly effective. A few days before Easter, a careful check showed less than twenty Negroes entering all the stores in the downtown area. Meanwhile, with the number of volunteers increasing daily, we were able to launch campaigns against a variety of additional objectives: kneel-ins at churches; sit-ins at the library; a march on the county building to mark the opening of a voter-registration drive. And all the time the jails were slowly but steadily filling up.

Birmingham residents of both races were surprised at the restraint of Connor's men at the beginning of the campaign. True, police dogs and clubs made their debut on Palm Sunday, but their appearance that day was brief and they quickly disappeared. What observers probably did not realize was that the commissioner was trying to take a leaf from the book of Police Chief Laurie Pritchett of Albany. Chief Pritchett felt that by directing his police to be nonviolent, he had discovered a new way to defeat the demonstrations. Mr. Connor, as it developed, was not to adhere to nonviolence long; the dogs were baying in kennels not far away; the hoses were primed. But that is another part of the story.

A second reason Bull Connor had held off at first was that he thought he had found another way out. This became evident on April 10, when the city government obtained a court injunction directing us to cease our activities until our right to demonstrate had been argued in court. The time had now come for us to counter their legal maneuver with a strategy of our own. Two days later, we did an audacious thing, something we had never done in any other crusade. We disobeyed a court order.

We did not take this radical step without prolonged and prayerful consideration. Planned, deliberate civil disobedience had been discussed as far back as the meeting at Harry Belafonte's apartment in March. There, in consultation with some of the closest friends of the movement, we had decided that if an injunction was issued to thwart our demonstrators, it would be our duty to violate it. To some, this will sound contradictory and morally indefensible. We, who contend for justice, and who oppose those who will not honor the law of the Supreme Court and the rulings of federal agencies, were saying that we would overtly violate a court order. Yet we felt that there were persuasive reasons for our position.

When the Supreme Court decision on school desegregation was handed down, leading segregationists vowed to thwart it by invoking "a century of litigation." There was more significance to this threat than many Americans imagined. The injunction method has now become the leading instrument of the South to block the direct-action civil-rights drive and to prevent Negro citizens and their white allies from engaging in peaceable assembly, a right guaranteed by the First Amendment. You initiate a nonviolent demonstration. The power structure secures an injunction against you. It can conceivably take two or three years before any disposition of the case is made. The Alabama courts are notorious for "sitting on" cases of this nature. This has been a maliciously effective, pseudo-legal way of breaking the back of legitimate moral protest.

We had anticipated that this procedure would be used in Birmingham. It had been invoked in Montgomery to outlaw our car pool during the bus boycott. It had destroyed the protest movement in Talladega, Alabama. It had torpedoed our effort in Albany, Georgia. It had routed the N.A.A.C.P. from the state of Alabama. We decided, therefore, knowing well what the consequences would be and prepared to accept them, that we had no choice but to violate such an injunction.

When the injunction was issued in Birmingham, our failure to obey it bewildered our opponents. They did not know what to do. We did not hide our intentions. In fact, I announced our plan to the press, pointing out that we were not anarchists advocating lawlessness, but that it was obvious to us that the courts of Alabama had misused the judicial process in order to perpetuate injustice and segregation. Consequently, we could not, in good conscience, obey their findings.

I intended to be one of the first to set the example of civil disobedience. Ten days after the demonstrations began, between four and five hundred people had gone to jail; some had been released on bail, but about three hundred remained. Now that the job of unifying the Negro community had been accomplished, my time had come. We decided that Good Friday, because of its symbolic significance, would be the day that Ralph Abernathy and I would present our bodies as personal witnesses in this crusade.

Soon after we announced our intention to lead a demonstration on April 12 and submit to arrest, we received a message so distressing that it threatened to ruin the movement. Late Thursday night, the bondsman who had been furnishing bail for the demonstrators notified us that he would be unable to continue. The city had notified him that his financial assets were insufficient. Obviously, this was another move on the part of the city to hurt our cause.

It was a serious blow. We had used up all the money we had on hand for cash bonds. There were our people in jail, for whom we had a moral responsibility. Fifty more were to go in with Ralph and me. This would be the largest single group to be arrested to date. Without bail facilities, how could we guarantee their eventual release?

Good Friday morning, early, I sat in Room 30 of the Gaston Motel discussing this crisis with twenty-four key people. As we talked, a sense of doom began to pervade the room. I looked about me and saw that, for the first time, our most dedicated and devoted leaders were overwhelmed by a feeling of hopelessness. No one knew what to say, for no one knew what to do. Finally someone spoke up and, as he spoke, I could see that he was giving voice to what was on everyone's mind.

"Martin," he said, "this means you can't go to jail. We need money. We need a lot of money. We need it now. You are the only one who has the contacts to get it. If you go to jail, we are lost. The battle of Birmingham is lost."

I sat there, conscious of twenty-four pairs of eyes. I thought about the people in jail. I thought about the Birmingham Negroes already lining the streets of the city, waiting to see me put into practice what I had so passionately preached. How could my failure now to submit to arrest be explained to the local community? What would be the verdict of the country about a man who had encouraged hundreds of people to make a stunning sacrifice and then excused himself?

Then my mind began to race in the opposite direction. Suppose I went to jail? What would happen to the three hundred? Where would the money come from to assure their release? What would happen to our campaign? Who would be willing to follow us into jail, not knowing when or whether he would ever walk out once more into the Birmingham sunshine?

I sat in the midst of the deepest quiet I have ever felt, with two dozen others in the room. There comes a time in the atmosphere of leadership when a man surrounded by loyal friends and allies realizes he has come face to face with himself. I was alone in that crowded room.

I walked to another room in the back of the suite, and stood in the center of the floor. I think I was standing also at the center of all that my life had brought me to be. I thought of the twenty-four people, waiting in the next room. I thought of the three hundred, waiting in prison. I thought of the Birmingham Negro community, waiting. Then my mind leaped beyond the Gaston Motel, past the city jail, past city lines and state lines, and I thought of twenty million black people who dreamed that someday they might be able to cross the Red Sea of injustice and find their way to the promised land of integration and freedom. There was no more room for doubt.

I pulled off my shirt and pants, got into work clothes and went back to the other room to tell them I had decided to go to jail.

"I don't know what will happen; I don't know where the money will come from. But I have to make a faith act."

I turned to Ralph Abernathy.

"I know you want to be in your pulpit on Easter Sunday, Ralph. But I am asking you to go with me."

As Ralph stood up without hesitation, we all linked hands, and twenty-five voices in Room 30 at the Gaston Motel in Birmingham, Alabama, chanted the battle hymn of our movement: "We Shall Overcome."

We rode from the motel to the Zion Hill church, where the march would begin. Many hundreds of Negroes had turned out to see us, and great hope grew within me as I saw those faces smiling approval as we passed. It seemed that every Birmingham police officer had been sent into the area. Leaving the church, where we were joined by the rest of our group of fifty, we started down the forbidden streets that lead to the downtown sector. It was a beautiful march. We were allowed to walk farther than the police had ever permitted before. We walked for seven or eight blocks. All along the way Negroes lined the streets. We were singing, and they were joining in. Occasionally the singing from the sidewalks was interspersed with bursts of applause.

As we neared the downtown area, Bull Connor ordered his men to arrest us. Ralph and I were hauled off by two muscular policemen, clutching the backs of our shirts in handfuls. All the others were promptly arrested. In jail Ralph and I were separated from everyone else, and later from each other.

For more than twenty-four hours I was held incommunicado, in solitary confinement. No one was permitted to visit me, not even my lawyers. Those were the longest, most frustrating and bewildering hours I have lived. Having no contact of any kind, I was besieged with worry. How was the movement faring? Where would Fred and the other leaders get the money to have our demonstrators released? What was happening to morale in the Negro community?

I suffered no physical brutality at the hands of my jailers. Some of the prison personnel were surly and abusive, but that was to be expected in southern prisons. Solitary confinement, however, was brutal enough. In the mornings the sun would rise, sending shafts of light through the window high in the narrow cell which was my home. You will never know the meaning of utter darkness until you have lain in such a dungeon, knowing that sunlight is streaming overhead and still seeing only darkness below. You might have thought I was in the grip of a fantasy brought on by worry. I did worry. But there was more to the blackness than a phenomenon conjured up by a worried mind. Whatever the cause, the fact remained that I could not see the light.

When I had left my Atlanta home some days before, my wife, Coretta, had just given birth to our fourth child. As happy as we were about the new little girl, Coretta was disappointed that her condition would not allow her to accompany me. She had been my strength and inspiration during the terror of Montgomery. She had been active in Albany, Georgia, and was preparing to go to jail with the wives of other civil-rights leaders there, just before the campaign ended.

Now, not only was she confined to our home, but

she was denied even the consolation of a telephone call from her husband. On the Monday following our jailing, she decided she must do something. Remembering the call that John Kennedy had made to her when I was jailed in Georgia during the 1960 election campaign, she placed a call to the president. Within a few minutes, his brother, Attorney General Robert Kennedy, phoned back. She told him that she had learned I was in solitary confinement and was afraid for my safety. The attorney general promised to do everything he could to have my situation eased. A few hours later President Kennedy himself called Coretta from Palm Beach, and assured her that he would look into the matter immediately. Apparently the president and his brother placed calls to officials in Birmingham; for immediately after Coretta heard from them, my jailers asked if I wanted to call her. After the president's intervention, conditions changed considerably.

Meanwhile, on Easter Sunday afternoon, two of our attorneys, Orzell Billingsley and Arthur Shores, had been allowed to visit me. They told me that Clarence B. Jones, my friend and lawyer, would be coming in from New York the following day. When they left, none of the questions tormenting me had been answered; but when Clarence Jones arrived the next day, before I could even tell him how happy I was to see him, he said a few words that lifted a thousand pounds from my heart:

"Harry Belafonte has been able to raise fifty thousand dollars for bail bonds. It is available immediately. And he says that whatever else you need, he will raise it."

I found it hard to say what I felt. Jones's message had brought me more than relief from the immediate concern about money; more than gratitude for the loyalty of friends far away; more than confirmation that the life of the movement could not be snuffed out. What silenced me was a profound sense of awe. I was aware of a feeling that had been present all along below the surface of consciousness, pressed down under the weight of concern for the movement: I had never been truly in solitary confinement; God's companionship does not stop at the door of a jail cell. I don't know whether the sun was shining at that moment. But I know that once again I could see the light.

V

*Letter from Birmingham Jail**

April 16, 1963

MY DEAR FELLOW CLERGYMEN:

While confined here in the Birmingham city jail, I
came across your recent statement calling my present
activities "unwise and untimely." Seldom do I pause to
answer criticism of my work and ideas. If I sought
to answer all the criticisms that cross my desk, my sec-
retaries would have little time for anything other than
such correspondence in the course of the day, and I
would have no time for constructive work. But since
I feel that you are men of genuine good will and that
your criticisms are sincerely set forth, I want to try to
answer your statement in what I hope will be patient
and reasonable terms.

---

*Author's Note: This response to a published statement by eight
fellow clergymen from Alabama (Bishop C. C. J. Carpenter, Bishop
Joseph A. Durick, Rabbi Hilton L. Grafman, Bishop Paul Hardin,
Bishop Holan B. Harmon, the Reverend George M. Murray, the Reverend Edward V. Ramage and the Reverend Earl Stallings) was com-
posed under somewhat constricting circumstances. Begun on the margins
of the newspaper in which the statement appeared while I was in jail, the
letter was continued on scraps of writing paper supplied by a friendly

I think I should indicate why I am here in Birmingham, since you have been influenced by the view which argues against "outsiders coming in." I have the honor of serving as president of the Southern Christian Leadership Conference, an organization operating in every southern state, with headquarters in Atlanta, Georgia. We have some eighty-five affiliated organizations across the South, and one of them is the Alabama Christian Movement for Human Rights. Frequently we share staff, educational and financial resources with our affiliates. Several months ago the affiliate here in Birmingham asked us to be on call to engage in a nonviolent direct-action program if such were deemed necessary. We readily consented, and when the hour came we lived up to our promise. So I, along with several members of my staff, am here because I was invited here. I am here because I have organizational ties here.

But more basically, I am in Birmingham because injustice is here. Just as the prophets of the eighth century B.C. left their villages and carried their "thus saith the Lord" far beyond the boundaries of their home towns, and just as the Apostle Paul left his village of Tarsus and carried the gospel of Jesus Christ to the far corners of the Greco-Roman world, so am I compelled to carry the gospel of freedom beyond my own home town. Like Paul, I must constantly respond to the Macedonian call for aid.

Moreover, I am cognizant of the interrelatedness of

Negro trusty, and concluded on a pad my attorneys were eventually permitted to leave me. Although the text remains in substance unaltered, I have indulged in the author's prerogative of polishing it for publication.

all communities and states. I cannot sit idly by in Atlanta and not be concerned about what happens in Birmingham. Injustice anywhere is a threat to justice everywhere. We are caught in an inescapable network of mutuality, tied in a single garment of destiny. Whatever affects one directly, affects all indirectly. Never again can we afford to live with the narrow, provincial "outside agitator" idea. Anyone who lives inside the United States can never be considered an outsider anywhere within its bounds.

You deplore the demonstrations taking place in Birmingham. But your statement, I am sorry to say, fails to express a similar concern for the conditions that brought about the demonstrations. I am sure that none of you would want to rest content with the superficial kind of social analysis that deals merely with effects and does not grapple with underlying causes. It is unfortunate that demonstrations are taking place in Birmingham, but it is even more unfortunate that the city's white power structure left the Negro community with no alternative.

In any nonviolent campaign there are four basic steps: collection of the facts to determine whether injustices exist; negotiation; self-purification; and direct action. We have gone through all these steps in Birmingham. There can be no gainsaying the fact that racial injustice engulfs this community. Birmingham is probably the most thoroughly segregated city in the United States. Its ugly record of brutality is widely known. Negroes have experienced grossly unjust treatment in the courts. There have been more unsolved bombings of Negro homes and churches in Birmingham than in any other city in the nation. These are the hard, brutal facts of the case. On the basis of these conditions, Negro leaders sought to negotiate with the city fathers. But the latter consistently refused to engage in good-faith negotiation.

Then, last September, came the opportunity to talk with leaders of Birmingham's economic community. In the course of the negotiations, certain promises were made by the merchants—for example, to remove the stores' humiliating racial signs. On the basis of these promises, the Reverend Fred Shuttlesworth and the leaders of the Alabama Christian Movement for Human Rights agreed to a moratorium on all demonstrations. As the weeks and months went by, we realized that we were the victims of a broken promise. A few signs, briefly removed, returned; the others remained.

As in so many past experiences, our hopes had been blasted, and the shadow of deep disappointment settled upon us. We had no alternative except to prepare for direct action, whereby we would present our very bodies as a means of laying our case before the conscience of the local and the national community. Mindful of the difficulties involved, we decided to undertake a process of self-purification. We began a series of workshops on nonviolence, and we repeatedly asked ourselves: "Are you able to accept blows without retaliating?" "Are you able to endure the ordeal of jail?" We decided to schedule our direct-action program for the Easter season, realizing that except for Christmas, this is the main shopping period of the year. Knowing that a strong economic-withdrawal program would be the by-product of direct action, we felt that this would be the best time to bring pressure to bear on the merchants for the needed change.

Then it occurred to us that Birmingham's mayoralty election was coming up in March, and we speedily decided to postpone action until after election day. When we discovered that the Commissioner of Public Safety, Eugene "Bull" Connor, had piled up enough votes to be in the run-off, we decided again to postpone action until the day after the run-off so that the demonstrations could not be used to cloud the issues. Like many others, we waited to see Mr. Connor defeated, and to this end we endured postponement after postponement. Having aided in this community need, we felt that our direct-action program could be delayed no longer.

You may well ask: "Why direct action? Why sit-ins, marches and so forth? Isn't negotiation a better path?" You are quite right in calling for negotiation. Indeed, this is the very purpose of direct action. Nonviolent direct action seeks to create such a crisis and foster such a tension that a community which has constantly refused to negotiate is forced to confront the issue. It seeks so to dramatize the issue that it can no longer be ignored. My citing the creation of tension as part of the work of the nonviolent-resister may sound rather shocking. But I must confess that I am not afraid of the word "tension." I have earnestly opposed violent tension, but there is a type of constructive, nonviolent tension which is necessary for growth. Just as Socrates felt that it was necessary to create a tension in the mind so that individuals could rise from the bondage of myths and half-truths to the unfettered realm of creative analysis and objective appraisal, so must we see the need for nonviolent gadflies to create the kind of tension in society that will help men rise from the dark depths of prejudice and racism to the majestic heights of understanding and brotherhood.

The purpose of our direct-action program is to create a situation so crisis-packed that it will inevitably open the door to negotiation. I therefore concur with you in your call for negotiation. Too long has our beloved Southland been bogged down in a tragic effort to live in monologue rather than dialogue.

One of the basic points in your statement is that the action that I and my associates have taken in Birmingham is untimely. Some have asked: "Why didn't you give the new city administration time to act?" The only answer that I can give to this query is that the new Birmingham administration must be prodded about as much as the outgoing one, before it will act. We are sadly mistaken if we feel that the election of Albert Boutwell as mayor will bring the millennium to Birmingham. While Mr. Boutwell is a much more gentle person than Mr. Connor, they are both segregationists, dedicated to maintenance of the status quo. I have hope that Mr. Boutwell will be reasonable enough to see the futility of massive resistance to desegregation. But he will not see this without pressure from devotees of civil rights. My friends, I must say to you that we have not made a single gain in civil rights without determined legal and nonviolent pressure. Lamentably, it is an historical fact that privileged groups seldom give up their privileges voluntarily. Individuals may see the moral light and voluntarily give up their unjust posture; but, as Reinhold Niebuhr has reminded us, groups tend to be more immoral than individuals.

We know through painful experience that freedom is never voluntarily given by the oppressor; it must be demanded by the oppressed. Frankly, I have yet to engage in a direct-action campaign that was "well timed" in the view of those who have not suffered unduly from the disease of segregation. For years now I have heard the word "Wait!" It rings in the ear of every Negro with piercing familiarity. This "Wait" has almost always meant "Never." We must come to see, with one of our distinguished jurists, that "justice too long delayed is justice denied."

We have waited for more than 340 years for our constitutional and God-given rights. The nations of Asia and Africa are moving with jetlike speed toward gaining political independence, but we still creep at horse-and-buggy pace toward gaining a cup of coffee at a lunch counter. Perhaps it is easy for those who have never felt the stinging darts of segregation to say, "Wait." But when you have seen vicious mobs lynch your mothers and fathers at will and drown your sisters and brothers at whim; when you have seen hate-filled policemen curse, kick and even kill your black brothers and sisters; when you see the vast majority of your twenty million Negro brothers smothering in an airtight cage of poverty in the midst of an affluent society; when you suddenly find your tongue twisted and your speech stammering as you seek to explain to your six-year-old daughter why she can't go to the public amusement park that has just been advertised on television, and see tears welling up in her eyes when she is told that Funtown is closed to colored children, and see ominous clouds of inferiority beginning to form in her little mental sky, and see her beginning to distort her personality by developing an unconscious bitterness toward white people; when you have to concoct an answer for a five-year-old son who is asking: "Daddy, why do white people treat colored people so mean?"; when you take a cross-country drive and find it necessary to sleep night after night in the uncomfortable corners of your automobile because no motel will accept you; when you are humiliated day in and day out by nagging signs reading "white" and "colored"; when your first name becomes "nigger," your middle name becomes "boy" (however old you are) and your last name becomes "John," and your wife and mother are never given the respected title "Mrs."; when you are harried by day and haunted by night by the fact that you are a Negro, living constantly at tiptoe stance, never quite knowing what to expect next, and are plagued with inner fears and outer resentments; when you are forever fighting a degenerating sense of "nobodiness"—then you will understand why we find it difficult to wait. There comes a time when the cup of endurance runs over, and men are no longer willing to be plunged into the abyss of despair. I hope, sirs, you can understand our legitimate and unavoidable impatience.

You express a great deal of anxiety over our willingness to break laws. This is certainly a legitimate concern. Since we so diligently urge people to obey the Supreme Court's decision of 1954 outlawing segregation in the public schools, at first glance it may seem rather paradoxical for us consciously to break laws. One may well ask: "How can you advocate breaking some laws and obeying others?" The answer lies in the fact that there are two types of laws: just and unjust. I would be the first to advocate obeying just laws. One has not only a legal but a moral responsibility to obey just laws. Conversely, one has a moral responsibility to disobey unjust laws. I would agree with St. Augustine that "an unjust law is no law at all."

Now, what is the difference between the two? How does one determine whether a law is just or unjust? A just law is a man-made code that squares with the moral law or the law of God. An unjust law is a code that is out of harmony with the moral law. To put it in the terms of St. Thomas Aquinas: An unjust law is a human law that is not rooted in eternal law and natural law. Any law that uplifts human personality is just. Any law that degrades human personality is unjust. All segregation statutes are unjust because segregation distorts the soul and damages the personality. It gives the segregator a false sense of superiority and the segregated a false sense of inferiority. Segregation, to use the terminology of the Jewish philosopher Martin Buber, substitutes an "I-it" relationship for an "I-thou" relationship and ends up relegating persons to the status of things. Hence segregation is not only politically, economically and sociologically unsound, it is morally wrong and sinful. Paul Tillich has said that sin is separation. Is not segregation an existential expression of man's tragic separation, his awful estrangement, his terrible sinfulness? Thus it is that I can urge men to obey the 1954 decision of the Supreme Court, for it is morally right; and I can urge them to disobey segregation ordinances, for they are morally wrong.

Let us consider a more concrete example of just and unjust laws. An unjust law is a code that a numerical or power majority group compels a minority group to obey but does not make binding on itself. This is *difference* made legal. By the same token, a just law is a code that a majority compels a minority to follow and that it is willing to follow itself. This is *sameness* made legal.

Let me give another explanation. A law is unjust if it is inflicted on a minority that, as a result of being denied the right to vote, had no part in enacting or devising the law. Who can say that the legislature of Alabama which set up that state's segregation laws was democratically elected? Throughout Alabama all sorts of devious methods are used to prevent Negroes from becoming registered voters, and there are some counties in which, even though Negroes constitute a majority of the population, not a single Negro is registered. Can any law enacted under such circumstances be considered democratically structured?

Sometimes a law is just on its face and unjust in its application. For instance, I have been arrested on a charge of parading without a permit. Now, there is nothing wrong in having an ordinance which requires a permit for a parade. But such an ordinance becomes unjust when it is used to maintain segregation and to deny citizens the First-Amendment privilege of peaceful assembly and protest.

I hope you are able to see the distinction I am trying to point out. In no sense do I advocate evading or defying the law, as would the rabid segregationist.

That would lead to anarchy. One who breaks an unjust law must do so openly, lovingly, and with a willingness to accept the penalty. I submit that an individual who breaks a law that conscience tells him is unjust, and who willingly accepts the penalty of imprisonment in order to arouse the conscience of the community over its injustice, is in reality expressing the highest respect for law.

Of course, there is nothing new about this kind of civil disobedience. It was evidenced sublimely in the refusal of Shadrach, Meshach and Abednego to obey the laws of Nebuchadnezzar, on the ground that a higher moral law was at stake. It was practiced superbly by the early Christians, who were willing to face hungry lions and the excruciating pain of chopping blocks rather than submit to certain unjust laws of the Roman Empire. To a degree, academic freedom is a reality today because Socrates practiced civil disobedience. In our own nation, the Boston Tea Party represented a massive act of civil disobedience.

We should never forget that everything Adolf Hitler did in Germany was "legal" and everything the Hungarian freedom fighters did in Hungary was "illegal." It was "illegal" to aid and comfort a Jew in Hitler's Germany. Even so, I am sure that, had I lived in Germany at the time, I would have aided and comforted my Jewish brothers. If today I lived in a Communist country where certain principles dear to the Christian faith are suppressed, I would openly advocate disobeying that country's antireligious laws.

I must make two honest confessions to you, my Christian and Jewish brothers. First, I must confess that over the past few years I have been gravely disappointed with the white moderate. I have almost reached the regrettable conclusion that the Negro's great stumbling block in his stride toward freedom is not the White Citizens' Counciler or the Ku Klux Klanner, but the white moderate, who is more devoted to "order" than to justice; who prefers a negative peace which is the absence of tension to a positive peace which is the presence of justice; who constantly says: "I agree with you in the goal you seek, but I cannot agree with your methods of direct action"; who paternalistically believes he can set the timetable for another man's freedom; who lives by a mythical concept of time and who constantly advises the Negro to wait for a "more convenient season." Shallow understanding from people of good will is more frustrating than absolute misunderstanding from people of ill will. Lukewarm acceptance is much more bewildering than outright rejection.

I had hoped that the white moderate would understand that law and order exist for the purpose of establishing justice and that when they fail in this purpose they become the dangerously structured dams that block the flow of social progress. I had hoped that the white moderate would understand that the present tension in the South is a necessary phase of the transition from an obnoxious negative peace, in which the Negro passively accepted his unjust plight, to a substantive and positive peace, in which all men will respect the dignity and worth of human personality. Actually, we who engage in nonviolent direct action are not the creators of tension. We merely bring to the surface the hidden tension that is already alive. We bring it out in the open, where it can be seen and dealt with. Like a boil that can never be cured so long as it is covered up but must be opened with all its ugliness to the natural medicines of air and light, injustice must be exposed, with all the tension its exposure creates, to the light of human conscience and the air of national opinion before it can be cured.

In your statement you assert that our actions, even though peaceful, must be condemned because they precipitate violence. But is this a logical assertion? Isn't this like condemning a robbed man because his possession of money precipitated the evil act of robbery? Isn't this like condemning Socrates because his unswerving commitment to truth and his philosophical inquiries precipitated the act by the misguided populace in which they made him drink hemlock? Isn't this like condemning Jesus because his unique God-consciousness and never-ceasing devotion to God's will precipitated the evil act of crucifixion? We must come to see that, as the federal courts have consistently affirmed, it is wrong to urge an individual to cease his efforts to gain his basic constitutional rights because the quest may precipitate violence. Society must protect the robbed and punish the robber.

I had also hoped that the white moderate would reject the myth concerning time in relation to the struggle for freedom. I have just received a letter from a white brother in Texas. He writes: "All Christians know that the colored people will receive equal rights eventually, but it is possible that you are in too great a religious hurry. It has taken Christianity almost two thousand years to accomplish what it has. The teachings of Christ take time to come to earth." Such an attitude stems from a tragic misconception of time, from the strangely irrational notion that there is something in the very flow of time that will inevitably cure all ills. Actually, time itself is neutral; it can be used either destructively or constructively. More and more I feel that the people of ill will have used time much more effectively than have the people of good will. We will have to repent in this generation not merely for the hateful words and actions of the bad people but for the appalling silence of the good people. Human progress never rolls in on wheels of inevitability; it comes through the tireless efforts of men willing to be coworkers with God, and without this hard work, time itself becomes an ally of the forces of social stagnation. We must use time creatively, in the knowledge that the time is always ripe to do right. Now is the time to make real the promise of democracy and transform our pending national elegy into a creative psalm of brotherhood. Now is the time to lift our national policy from the quicksand of racial injustice to the solid rock of human dignity.

You speak of our activity in Birmingham as extreme. At first I was rather disappointed that fellow clergymen would see my nonviolent efforts as those of an extremist. I began thinking about the fact that I stand in the middle of two opposing forces in the Negro community. One is a force of complacency, made up in part of Negroes who, as a result of long years of oppression, are so drained of self-respect and a sense of "somebodiness" that they have adjusted to segregation; and in part of a few middle-class Negroes who, because of a degree of academic and economic secu-

Abernathy, left, and King are taken by a policeman after they led
a line of demonstrators into the business section of Birmingham.

Abernathy and King are arrested at the conclusion of a march
in considered defiance of the injunction.

Fred Shuttlesworth leads Birmingham marchers in prayer before their arrest.

From left: Ralph Abernathy, King, and Fred Shuttlesworth read a court order enjoining further demonstrations.

Eugene "Bull" Connor, commissioner of public safety,
leads his men into action.

Birmingham police "defend
the public safety" against a
female demonstrator.

A six-year-old girl waits for a policeman to take her name before she is led away to a waiting police truck. More than 450 schoolchildren were arrested for protesting against racial discrimination.

When the jails overflow, following the massive desegregation protests of the past three days, young marchers are held in custody at the fairgrounds in Birmingham. The teenagers are among an estimated one thousand people in custody.

Firefighters turn their power hoses on civil rights demonstrators in Birmingham.

The home of Rev. A. D. King, brother of Dr. Martin Luther King, Jr., is a shambles after it was dynamited in Birmingham.

Four months after the truce: from inside the bombed-out
Sixteenth Street Baptist Church, where four African American
Sunday school students were killed.

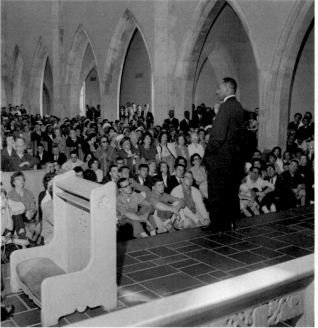

King reports to an
overflow audience
at St. Paul's Episcopal
Church in Cleveland
in an effort to raise
money for the drive
against segregation.

Six leaders of the nation's largest national black organizations met in New York's Roosevelt Hotel to discuss plans for a civil rights march on Washington, D.C. From left: John Lewis, Whitney Young, Jr., A. Philip Randolph, King, James Farmer, and Roy Wilkins.

The leaders of the March on Washington lock arms as they lead the way along Constitution Avenue. King is at center, seventh from the right; on the extreme right are march director A. Philip Randolph and Roy Wilkins, executive secretary of the NAACP.

A rare moment at home in Atlanta: King, Coretta,
and their children.

rity and because in some ways they profit by segregation, have become insensitive to the problems of the
masses. The other force is one of bitterness and hatred,
and it comes perilously close to advocating violence. It
is expressed in the various black nationalist groups that
are springing up across the nation, the largest and best
known being Elijah Muhammad's Muslim movement.
Nourished by the Negro's frustration over the continued existence of racial discrimination, this movement
is made up of people who have lost faith in America,
who have absolutely repudiated Christianity, and who
have concluded that the white man is an incorrigible
"devil."

I have tried to stand between these two forces, saying that we need emulate neither the "do-nothingism"
of the complacent nor the hatred and despair of the
black nationalist. For there is the more excellent way of
love and nonviolent protest. I am grateful to God that,
through the influence of the Negro church, the way of
nonviolence became an integral part of our struggle.

If this philosophy had not emerged, by now many
streets of the South would, I am convinced, be flow-
ing with blood. And I am further convinced that if our
white brothers dismiss as "rabble-rousers" and "outside
agitators" those of us who employ nonviolent direct action, and if they refuse to support our nonviolent efforts, millions of Negroes will, out of frustration and
despair, seek solace and security in black-nationalist
ideologies—a development that would inevitably lead
to a frightening racial nightmare.

Oppressed people cannot remain oppressed forever.
The yearning for freedom eventually manifests itself,

and that is what has happened to the American Negro. Something within has reminded him of his birthright of freedom, and something without has reminded him that it can be gained. Consciously or unconsciously, he has been caught up by the *Zeitgeist*, and with his black brothers of Africa and his brown and yellow brothers of Asia, South America and the Caribbean, the United States Negro is moving with a sense of great urgency toward the promised land of racial justice. If one recognizes this vital urge that has engulfed the Negro community, one should readily understand why public demonstrations are taking place. The Negro has many pent-up resentments and latent frustrations, and he must release them. So let him march; let him make prayer pilgrimages to the city hall; let him go on freedom rides—and try to understand why he must do so. If his repressed emotions are not released in nonviolent ways, they will seek expression through violence; this is not a threat but a fact of history. So I have not said to my people: "Get rid of your discontent." Rather, I have tried to say that this normal and healthy discontent can be channeled into the creative outlet of nonviolent direct action. And now this approach is being termed extremist.

But though I was initially disappointed at being categorized as an extremist, as I continued to think about the matter I gradually gained a measure of satisfaction from the label. Was not Jesus an extremist for love: "Love your enemies, bless them that curse you, do good to them that hate you, and pray for them which despitefully use you, and persecute you." Was not Amos an extremist for justice: "Let justice roll down like waters and righteousness like an ever-flowing stream." Was not Paul an extremist for the Christian gospel: "I bear in my body the marks of the Lord Jesus." Was not Martin Luther an extremist: "Here I stand; I cannot do otherwise, so help me God." And John Bunyan: "I will stay in jail to the end of my days before I make a butchery of my conscience." And Abraham Lincoln: "This nation cannot survive half slave and half free." And Thomas Jefferson: "We hold these truths to be self-evident, that all men are created equal . . ." So the question is not whether we will be extremists, but what kind of extremists we will be. Will we be extremists for hate or for love? Will we be extremists for the preservation of injustice or for the extension of justice? In that dramatic scene on Calvary's hill three men were crucified. We must never forget that all three were crucified for the same crime—the crime of extremism. Two were extremists for immorality, and thus fell below their environment. The other, Jesus Christ, was an extremist for love, truth and goodness, and thereby rose above his environment. Perhaps the South, the nation and the world are in dire need of creative extremists.

I had hoped that the white moderate would see this need. Perhaps I was too optimistic; perhaps I expected too much. I suppose I should have realized that few members of the oppressor race can understand the deep groans and passionate yearnings of the oppressed race, and still fewer have the vision to see that injustice must be rooted out by strong, persistent and determined action. I am thankful, however, that some of our white brothers in the South have grasped the meaning of this social revolution and committed themselves to it.

They are still all too few in quantity, but they are big in quality. Some—such as Ralph McGill, Lillian Smith, Harry Golden, James McBride Dabbs, Ann Braden and Sarah Patton Boyle—have written about our struggle in eloquent and prophetic terms. Others have marched with us down nameless streets of the South. They have languished in filthy, roach-infested jails, suffering the abuse and brutality of policemen who view them as "dirty nigger-lovers." Unlike so many of their moderate brothers and sisters, they have recognized the urgency of the moment and sensed the need for powerful "action" antidotes to combat the disease of segregation.

Let me take note of my other major disappointment. I have been so greatly disappointed with the white church and its leadership. Of course, there are some notable exceptions. I am not unmindful of the fact that each of you has taken some significant stands on this issue. I commend you, Reverend Stallings, for your Christian stand on this past Sunday, in welcoming Negroes to your worship service on a nonsegregated basis. I commend the Catholic leaders of this state for integrating Spring Hill College several years ago.

But despite these notable exceptions, I must honestly reiterate that I have been disappointed with the church. I do not say this as one of those negative critics who can always find something wrong with the church. I say this as a minister of the gospel, who loves the church; who was nurtured in its bosom; who has been sustained by its spiritual blessings and who will remain true to it as long as the cord of life shall lengthen.

When I was suddenly catapulted into the leadership of the bus protest in Montgomery, Alabama, a few years ago, I felt we would be supported by the white church. I felt that the white ministers, priests and rabbis of the South would be among our strongest allies. Instead, some have been outright opponents, refusing to understand the freedom movement and misrepresenting its leaders; all too many others have been more cautious than courageous and have remained silent behind the anesthetizing security of stained-glass windows.

In spite of my shattered dreams, I came to Birmingham with the hope that the white religious leadership of this community would see the justice of our cause and, with deep moral concern, would serve as the channel through which our just grievances could reach the power structure. I had hoped that each of you would understand. But again I have been disappointed.

I have heard numerous southern religious leaders admonish their worshipers to comply with a desegregation decision because it is the law, but I have longed to hear white ministers declare: "Follow this decree because integration is morally right and because the Negro is your brother." In the midst of blatant injustices inflicted upon the Negro, I have watched white churchmen stand on the sideline and mouth pious irrelevancies and sanctimonious trivialities. In the midst of a mighty struggle to rid our nation of racial and economic injustice, I have heard many ministers say: "Those are social issues, with which the gospel has no real concern." And I have watched many churches commit themselves to a completely otherworldly religion which makes a strange, un-Biblical distinction between body and soul, between the sacred and the secular.

I have traveled the length and breadth of Alabama,

Mississippi and all the other southern states. On sweltering summer days and crisp autumn mornings I have looked at the South's beautiful churches with their lofty spires pointing heavenward. I have beheld the impressive outlines of her massive religious-education buildings. Over and over I have found myself asking: "What kind of people worship here? Who is their God? Where were their voices when the lips of Governor Barnett dripped with words of interposition and nullification? Where were they when Governor Wallace gave a clarion call for defiance and hatred? Where were their voices of support when bruised and weary Negro men and women decided to rise from the dark dungeons of complacency to the bright hills of creative protest?"

Yes, these questions are still in my mind. In deep disappointment I have wept over the laxity of the church. But be assured that my tears have been tears of love. There can be no deep disappointment where there is not deep love. Yes, I love the church. How could I do otherwise? I am in the rather unique position of being the son, the grandson and the great-grandson of preachers. Yes, I see the church as the body of Christ. But, oh! How we have blemished and scarred that body through social neglect and through fear of being non-conformists.

There was a time when the church was very powerful—in the time when the early Christians rejoiced at being deemed worthy to suffer for what they believed. In those days the church was not merely a thermometer that recorded the ideas and principles of popular opinion; it was a thermostat that transformed the mores of society. Whenever the early Christians entered a town, the people in power became disturbed and immediately sought to convict the Christians for being "disturbers of the peace" and "outside agitators." But the Christians pressed on, in the conviction that they were "a colony of heaven," called to obey God rather than man. Small in number, they were big in commitment. They were too God-intoxicated to be "astronomically intimidated." By their effort and example they brought an end to such ancient evils as infanticide and gladiatorial contests.

Things are different now. So often the contemporary church is a weak, ineffectual voice with an uncertain sound. So often it is an archdefender of the status quo. Far from being disturbed by the presence of the church, the power structure of the average community is consoled by the church's silent—and often even vocal—sanction of things as they are.

But the judgment of God is upon the church as never before. If today's church does not recapture the sacrificial spirit of the early church, it will lose its authenticity, forfeit the loyalty of millions, and be dismissed as an irrelevant social club with no meaning for the twentieth century. Every day I meet young people whose disappointment with the church has turned into outright disgust.

Perhaps I have once again been too optimistic. Is organized religion too inextricably bound to the status quo to save our nation and the world? Perhaps I must turn my faith to the inner spiritual church, the church within the church, as the true *ekklesia* and the hope of the world. But again I am thankful to God that some noble souls from the ranks of organized religion have broken loose from the paralyzing chains of conformity and joined us as active partners in the struggle for freedom. They have left their secure congregations and walked the streets of Albany, Georgia, with us. They have gone down the highways of the South on tortuous rides for freedom. Yes, they have gone to jail with us. Some have been dismissed from their churches, have lost the support of their bishops and fellow ministers. But they have acted in the faith that right defeated is stronger than evil triumphant. Their witness has been the spiritual salt that has preserved the true meaning of the gospel in these troubled times. They have carved a tunnel of hope through the dark mountain of disappointment.

I hope the church as a whole will meet the challenge of this decisive hour. But even if the church does not come to the aid of justice, I have no despair about the future. I have no fear about the outcome of our struggle in Birmingham, even if our motives are at present misunderstood. We will reach the goal of freedom in Birmingham and all over the nation, because the goal of America is freedom. Abused and scorned though we may be, our destiny is tied up with America's destiny. Before the pilgrims landed at Plymouth, we were here. Before the pen of Jefferson etched the majestic words of the Declaration of Independence across the pages of history, we were here. For more than two centuries our forebears labored in this country without wages; they made cotton king; they built the homes of their masters while suffering gross injustice and shameful humiliation—and yet out of a bottomless vitality they continued to thrive and develop. If the inexpressible cruelties of slavery could not stop us, the opposition we now face will surely fail. We will win our freedom because the sacred heritage of our nation and the eternal will of God are embodied in our echoing demands.

Before closing I feel impelled to mention one other point in your statement that has troubled me profoundly. You warmly commended the Birmingham police force for keeping "order" and "preventing violence." I doubt that you would have so warmly commended the police force if you had seen its dogs sinking their teeth into unarmed, nonviolent Negroes. I doubt that you would so quickly commend the policemen if you were to observe their ugly and inhumane treatment of Negroes here in the city jail; if you were to watch them push and curse old Negro women and young Negro girls; if you were to see them slap and kick old Negro men and young boys; if you were to observe them, as they did on two occasions, refuse to give us food because we wanted to sing our grace together. I cannot join you in your praise of the Birmingham police department.

It is true that the police have exercised a degree of discipline in handling the demonstrators. In this sense they have conducted themselves rather "nonviolently" in public. But for what purpose? To preserve the evil system of segregation. Over the past few years I have consistently preached that nonviolence demands that the means we use must be as pure as the ends we seek. I have tried to make clear that it is wrong to use immoral means to attain moral ends. But now I must affirm that it is just as wrong, or perhaps even more so, to use moral means to preserve immoral ends. Perhaps Mr. Connor and his policemen have been rather nonviolent in public, as was Chief Pritchett in Albany, Georgia, but they have used the moral means of nonviolence to maintain the immoral end of racial injustice. As T. S. Eliot has said: "The last temptation is the greatest treason: To do the right deed for the wrong reason."

I wish you had commended the Negro sit-inners and demonstrators of Birmingham for their sublime courage, their willingness to suffer and their amazing discipline in the midst of great provocation. One day the South will recognize its real heroes. They will be the James Merediths, with the noble sense of purpose that enables them to face jeering and hostile mobs, and with the agonizing loneliness that characterizes the life of the pioneer. They will be old, oppressed, battered Negro women, symbolized in a seventy-two-year-old woman in Montgomery, Alabama, who rose up with a sense of dignity and with her people decided not to ride segregated buses, and who responded with un-grammatical profundity to one who inquired about her weariness: "My feets is tired, but my soul is at rest." They will be the young high school and college students, the young ministers of the gospel and a host of their elders, courageously and nonviolently sitting in at lunch counters and willingly going to jail for con-science' sake. One day the South will know that when these disinherited children of God sat down at lunch counters, they were in reality standing up for what is best in the American dream and for the most sacred values in our Judaeo-Christian heritage, thereby bring-ing our nation back to those great wells of democracy which were dug deep by the founding fathers in their formulation of the Constitution and the Declaration of Independence.

Never before have I written so long a letter. I'm afraid it is much too long to take your precious time. I can assure you that it would have been much shorter if I had been writing from a comfortable desk, but what else can one do when he is alone in a narrow jail cell other than write long letters, think long thoughts and pray long prayers?

If I have said anything in this letter that overstates the truth and indicates an unreasonable impatience, I beg you to forgive me. If I have said anything that understates the truth and indicates my having a patience that allows me to settle for anything less than brotherhood, I beg God to forgive me.

I hope this letter finds you strong in the faith. I also hope that circumstances will soon make it possible for me to meet each of you, not as an integrationist or a civil-rights leader but as a fellow clergyman and a Christian brother. Let us all hope that the dark clouds of racial prejudice will soon pass away and the deep fog of misunderstanding will be lifted from our fear-drenched communities, and in some not too distant tomorrow the radiant stars of love and brotherhood will shine over our great nation with all their scintillating beauty.

Yours for the cause of Peace and Brotherhood,

MARTIN LUTHER KING, JR.

VI

Black and White Together

After eight days of imprisonment, Ralph Abernathy and I accepted bond to come out of jail for two purposes. It was necessary for me to regain communication with the S.C.L.C. officers and our lawyers in order to map the strategy for the contempt cases that would be coming up shortly in the circuit court. Also, I had decided to put into operation a new phase of our campaign, which I felt would speed victory.

I called my staff together and repeated a conviction I had been voicing ever since the campaign began. If our drive was to be successful, we must involve the students of the community. In most of the recent direct-action crusades, it had been the young people who sparked the movement. But in Birmingham, of the first four or five hundred people who had submitted themselves to arrest, two-thirds had been adults. We had considered this a good thing at the time, for a really effective campaign incorporates a cross section of the community. But now it was time to enlist the young people in larger numbers. Even though we realized that involving teenagers and high-school students would bring down upon us a heavy fire of criticism, we felt that we needed this dramatic new dimension. Our people were demonstrating daily and going to jail in numbers, but we were still beating our heads against the brick wall of the city officials' stubborn resolve to maintain the status quo. Our fight, if won, would benefit people of all ages. But most of all we were inspired with a desire to give to our young a true sense of their own stake in freedom and justice. We believed they would have the courage to respond to our call.

James Bevel, Andy Young, Bernard Lee and Dorothy Cotton began visiting colleges and high schools in the area. They invited students to attend after-school meetings at churches. The word spread fast, and the response from Birmingham's youngsters exceeded our fondest dreams. By the fifties and by the hundreds, these youngsters attended mass meetings and training sessions. They listened eagerly as we talked of bringing freedom to Birmingham, not in some distant time, but right now. We taught them the philosophy of nonviolence. We challenged them to bring their exuberance, their youthful creativity, into the disciplined dedication of the movement. We found them eager to belong, hungry for participation in a significant social effort. Looking back, it is clear that the introduction of Birmingham's children into the campaign was one of the wisest moves we made. It brought a new impact to the crusade, and the impetus that we needed to win the struggle.

Immediately, of course, a cry of protest went up. Although by the end of April the attitude of the national press had changed considerably, so that the major media were according us sympathetic coverage, yet many deplored our "using" our children in this fashion. Where had these writers been, we wondered, during the centuries when our segregated social system had been misusing and abusing Negro children? Where had they been with their protective words when, down through the years, Negro infants were born into ghettos, taking their first breath of life in a social atmosphere where the fresh air of freedom was crowded out by the stench of discrimination?

The children themselves had the answer to the misguided sympathies of the press. One of the most ringing replies came from a child of no more than eight who walked with her mother one day in a demonstration. An amused policeman leaned down to her and said with mock gruffness: "What do you want?"

The child looked into his eyes, unafraid, and gave her answer.

"F'eedom," she said.

She could not even pronounce the word, but no Gabriel trumpet could have sounded a truer note.

Even children too young to march requested and earned a place in our ranks. Once when we sent out a call for volunteers, six tiny youngsters responded. Andy Young told them that they were not old enough to go to jail but that they could go to the library. "You won't get arrested there," he said, "but you might learn something." So these six small children marched off to the building in the white district, where, up to two weeks before, they would have been turned away at the door. Shyly but doggedly, they went to the children's room and sat down, and soon they were lost in their books. In their own way, they had struck a blow, for freedom.

The children understood the stakes they were fighting for. I think of one teenage boy whose father's devotion to the movement turned sour when he learned that his son had pledged himself to become a demonstrator. The father forbade his son to participate.

"Daddy," the boy said, "I don't want to disobey you, but I have made my pledge. If you try to keep me home, I will sneak off. If you think I deserve to be punished for that, I'll just have to take the punishment. For, you see, I'm not doing this only because I want to be free. I'm doing it also because I want freedom for you and Mama, and I want it to come before you die."

That father thought again, and gave his son his blessing.

The movement was blessed by the fire and excitement brought to it by young people such as these. And when Birmingham youngsters joined the march in numbers, an historic thing happened. For the first time in the civil-rights movement, we were able to put into effect the Gandhian principle: "Fill up the jails."

Jim Bevel had the inspiration of setting a "D" Day, when the students would go to jail in historic numbers. When that day arrived, young people converged on the Sixteenth Street Baptist Church in wave after wave. Altogether on "D" Day, May 2, more than a thousand young people demonstrated and went to jail. At one school, the principal gave orders to lock the gates to keep the students in. The youngsters climbed over the gates and ran toward freedom. The assistant superintendent of schools threatened them with expulsion, and still they came, day after day. At the height of the campaign, by conservative estimates, there were 2,500 demonstrators in jail at one time, a large proportion of them young people.

Serious as they were about what they were doing, these teenagers had that marvelous humor that arms the unarmed in the face of danger. Under their leaders, they took delight in confusing the police. A small decoy group would gather at one exit of the church, bringing policemen streaming in cars and on motorcycles. Before the officers knew what was happening, other groups, by the scores, would pour out of other exits and move, two by two, toward our goal in the downtown section.

Many arrived at their destination before the police could confront and arrest them. They sang as they marched and as they were loaded into the paddy wagons. The police ran out of paddy wagons and had to press sheriff's cars and school buses into service.

Watching those youngsters in Birmingham, I could not help remembering an episode in Montgomery during the bus boycott. Someone had asked an elderly woman why she was involved in our struggle.

"I'm doing it for my children and for my grandchildren," she had replied.

Seven years later, the children and grandchildren were doing it for themselves.

II

With the jails filling up and the scorching glare of national disapproval focused on Birmingham, Bull Connor abandoned his posture of nonviolence. The result was an ugliness too well known to Americans and to people all over the world. The newspapers of May 4 carried pictures of prostrate women, and policemen bending over them with raised clubs; of children marching up to the bared fangs of police dogs; of the terrible force of pressure hoses sweeping bodies into the streets.

This was the time of our greatest stress, and the courage and conviction of those students and adults made it our finest hour. We did not fight back, but we did not turn back. We did not give way to bitterness. Some few spectators, who had not been trained in the discipline of nonviolence, reacted to the brutality of the policemen by throwing rocks and bottles. But the demonstrators remained nonviolent. In the face of this resolution and bravery, the moral conscience of the nation was deeply stirred and, all over the country, our fight became the fight of decent Americans of all races and creeds.

The moral indignation which was spreading throughout the land; the sympathy created by the children; the growing involvement of the Negro community—all these factors were mingling to create a certain atmosphere inside our movement. It was a pride in progress and a conviction that we were going to win. It was a mounting optimism which gave us the feeling that the implacable barriers that confronted us were doomed and already beginning to crumble. We were advised, in the utmost confidence, that the white business structure was weakening under the adverse publicity, the pressure of our boycott, and a parallel falling-off of white buying.

Strangely enough, the masses of white citizens in Birmingham were not fighting us. This was one of the most amazing aspects of the Birmingham crusade. Only a year or so ago, had we begun such a campaign, Bull Connor would have had his job done for him by murderously angry white citizens. Now, however, the majority were maintaining a strictly hands-off policy. I do not mean to insinuate that they were in sympathy with our cause or that they boycotted stores because we did. I simply suggest that it is powerfully symbolic of shifting attitudes in the South that the majority of the white citizens of Birmingham remained neutral through our campaign. This neutrality added force to our feeling that we were on the road to victory.

On one dramatic occasion even Bull Connor's men were shaken. It was a Sunday afternoon, when several hundred Birmingham Negroes had determined to hold a prayer meeting near the city jail. They gathered at the New Pilgrim Baptist Church and began an orderly march. Bull Connor ordered out the police dogs and fire hoses. When the marchers approached the border between the white and Negro areas, Connor ordered them to turn back. The Reverend Charles Billups, who was leading the march, politely refused. Enraged, Bull Connor whirled on his men and shouted:

"Dammit. Turn on the hoses."

What happened in the next thirty seconds was one of the most fantastic events of the Birmingham story. Bull Connor's men, their deadly hoses poised for action, stood facing the marchers. The marchers, many of them on their knees, stared back, unafraid and unmoving. Slowly the Negroes stood up and began to advance. Connor's men, as though hypnotized, fell back, their hoses sagging uselessly in their hands while several hundred Negroes marched past them, without further interference, and held their prayer meeting as planned.

One more factor helped to encourage us in the belief that our goals were coming within reach. We had demonstrated in defiance of a civil injunction. For this act of disobedience, we had been cited for contempt. In Alabama, if you are cited for criminal contempt, you serve five days and that is the end of it. If you are cited for civil contempt, however, you figuratively hold the jailhouse keys in the palm of your hand. At any time, if you are willing to recant, you can earn release. If you do not recant, you can be held for the rest of your natural life.

Most of the demonstrators had been cited for criminal contempt. About ten of us, however, all leaders of the movement, had been cited for civil contempt. When we were first placed under this charge, I am certain that the Birmingham authorities believed we would back down rather than face the threat of indefinite imprisonment. But by the time we appeared in court late in April to answer the charges, all of Birmingham knew that we would never recant, even if we had to rot away in their jails. The city thus faced the prospect of putting us into jail for life. Confronted with the certain knowledge that we would not give in, the city attorney undoubtedly realized that he would be sentencing us to a martyrdom which must eventually turn the full force of national public opinion against Birmingham.

Abruptly the tactics were reversed. The civil-contempt charge was changed to the less stringent criminal-contempt charge, under which we were swiftly convicted on April 26. In addition, the judge announced that he would delay sentence and give us about twenty days to file an appeal. At this point there was little doubt in our minds that Birmingham's bastions of segregation were weakening.

III

Throughout the campaign, we had been seeking to establish some dialogue with the city leaders in an effort to negotiate on four major issues:

1. The desegregation of lunch counters, restrooms, fitting rooms and drinking fountains in variety and department stores.
2. The upgrading and hiring of Negroes on a non-discriminatory basis throughout the business and industrial community of Birmingham.
3. The dropping of all charges against jailed demonstrators.
4. The creation of a biracial committee to work out a timetable for desegregation in other areas of Birmingham life.

Even though pressure on Birmingham's business community was intense, there were stubborn men in its midst who seemed to feel they would rather see their own enterprises fail than sit across the table and negotiate with our leadership. However, when national pressure began to pile up on the White House, climaxing with the infamous day of May 3, the administration was forced to act. On May 4, the attorney general dispatched Burke Marshall, his chief civil-rights assistant, and Joseph F. Dolan, assistant deputy attorney general, to seek a truce in the tense racial situation. Though Marshall had no ultimate power to impose a solution, he had full authority to represent the president in the negotiations. It was one of the first times the federal government had taken so active a role in such circumstances.

I must confess that although I appreciated the fact that the administration had finally made a decisive move, I had some initial misgivings concerning Marshall's intentions. I was afraid that he had come to urge a "cooling off" period—to ask us to declare a one-sided truce as a condition to negotiations. To his credit, Marshall did not adopt such a position. Rather, he did an invaluable job of opening channels of communication between our leadership and the top people in the economic power structure. Said one staunch defender of segregation, after conferring with Marshall: "There is a man who listens. I had to listen back, and I guess I grew up a little."

With Burke Marshall as catalyst, we began to hold secret meetings with the Senior Citizens Committee. At these sessions, unpromising as they were at the outset, we laid the groundwork for the agreement that would eventually accord us all of our major demands.

Meanwhile, however, for several days violence swept through the streets of Birmingham. An armored car was added to Bull Connor's strange armament. And some Negroes, not trained in our nonviolent methods, again responded with bricks and bottles. On one of these days, when the pressure in Connor's hoses was so high that it peeled the bark off the trees, Fred Shuttlesworth was hurled by a blast of water against the side of a building. Suffering injuries in his chest, he was carried away in an ambulance. Connor, when told, responded in characteristic fashion. "I wish he'd been carried away in a hearse," he said. Fortunately, Shuttlesworth is resilient and though still in pain he was back at the conference table the next day.

Terrified by the very destructiveness brought on by their own acts, the city police appealed for state troopers to be brought into the area. Many of the white leaders now realized that something had to be done. Yet there were those among them who were still adamant. But one other incident was to occur that would transform recalcitrance into good faith. On Tuesday, May 7, the Senior Citizens Committee had assembled in a downtown building to discuss our demands. In the first hours of this meeting, they were so intransigent that Burke Marshall despaired of a pact. The atmosphere was charged with tension, and tempers were running high.

In this mood, these 125-odd business leaders adjourned for lunch. As they walked out on the street, an extraordinary sight met their eyes. On that day several thousand Negroes had marched on the town. The jails were so full that the police could only arrest a handful. There were Negroes on the sidewalks, in the streets, standing, sitting in the aisles of downtown stores. There were square blocks of Negroes, a veritable sea of black faces. They were committing no violence; they were just present and singing. Downtown Birmingham echoed to the strains of the freedom songs.

Astounded, those businessmen, key figures in a great city, suddenly realized that the movement could not be stopped. When they returned—from the lunch they were unable to get—one of the men who had been in the most determined opposition cleared his throat and said: "You know, I've been thinking this thing through. We ought to be able to work something out."

That admission marked the beginning of the end. Late that afternoon, Burke Marshall informed us that representatives from the business and industrial community wanted to meet with the movement leaders immediately to work out a settlement. After talking with these men for about three hours, we became convinced that they were negotiating in good faith. On the basis of this assurance we called a twenty-four-hour truce on Wednesday morning.

That day the president devoted the entire opening statement of his press conference to the Birmingham situation, emphasizing how vital it was that the problems be squarely faced and resolved and expressing encouragement that a dialogue now existed between the opposing sides. Even while the president spoke, the truce was briefly threatened when Ralph and I were suddenly clapped into jail on an old charge. Some of my associates, feeling that they had again been betrayed, put on their walking shoes and prepared to march. They were restrained, however; we were swiftly bailed out; and negotiations were resumed.

After talking all night Wednesday, and practically all day and night Thursday, we reached an accord. On Friday, May 10, this agreement was announced. It contained the following pledges:

1. The desegregation of lunch counters, restrooms, fitting rooms and drinking fountains, in planned stages within ninety days after signing.
2. The upgrading and hiring of Negroes on a non-discriminatory basis throughout the industrial community of Birmingham, to include hiring of Negroes as clerks and salesmen within sixty days after signing of the agreement—and the immediate appointment of a committee of business, industrial and professional leaders to implement an area-wide program for the acceleration of upgrading and employment of Negroes in job categories previously denied to them.
3. Official cooperation with the movement's legal representatives in working out the release of all jailed persons on bond or on their personal recognizance.
4. Through the Senior Citizens Committee or Chamber of Commerce, communications between Negro and white to be publicly established within two weeks after signing, in order to prevent the necessity of further demonstrations and protests.

Our troubles were not over. The announcement that a peace pact had been signed in Birmingham was flashed across the world by the hundred-odd foreign correspondents then covering the campaign on the crowded scene. It was headlined in the nation's press and heralded on network television. Segregationist forces within the city were consumed with fury. They vowed reprisals against the white businessmen who had "betrayed" them by capitulating to the cause of Negro equality. On Saturday night, they gave their brutal answer to the pact. Following a Ku Klux Klan meeting on the outskirts of town, the home of my brother, the Reverend A.D. King, was bombed. That same night a bomb was planted near the Gaston Motel, a bomb so placed as to kill or seriously wound anyone who might have been in Room 30—my room. Evidently the would-be assassins did not know I was in Atlanta that night.

The bombing had been well timed. The bars in the Negro district close at midnight, and the bombs exploded just as some of Birmingham's Saturday-night drinkers came out of the bars. Thousands of Negroes poured into the streets. Wyatt Walker, my brother and others urged them to go home, but they were not under the discipline of the movement and were in no mood to listen to counsels of peace. Fighting began. Stones were hurled at the police. Cars were wrecked and fires started. Whoever planted the bombs had *wanted* the Negroes to riot. They wanted the pact upset.

Governor George Wallace's state police and "conservation men" sealed off the Negro area and moved in with their bullies and pistols. They beat numerous innocent Negroes; among their acts of chivalry was the clubbing of the diminutive Anne Walker, Wyatt's wife, as she was about to enter her husband's quarters at the partially bombed-out Gaston Motel. They further distinguished themselves by beating Wyatt when he was attempting to drive back home after seeing his wife to the hospital.

I shall never forget the phone call my brother placed

to me in Atlanta that violent Saturday night. His home had just been destroyed. Several people had been injured at the motel. I listened as he described the erupting tumult and catastrophe in the streets of the city. Then, in the background as he talked, I heard a swelling burst of beautiful song. Feet planted in the rubble of debris, threatened by criminal violence and hatred, followers of the movement were singing "We Shall Overcome." I marveled that in a moment of such tragedy the Negro could still express himself with hope and with faith.

The following evening, a thoroughly aroused president told the nation that the federal government would not allow extremists to sabotage a fair and just pact. He ordered three thousand federal troops into position near Birmingham and made preparations to federalize the Alabama National Guard. This firm action stopped the troublemakers in their tracks.

Yet the segregationist die-hards were to attempt still once more to destroy the peace. On May 20 the headlines announced that more than a thousand students who had participated in the demonstrations had been either suspended or expelled by the city's Board of Education. I am convinced that this was another attempt to drive the Negro community to an unwise and impulsive move. The plot might have worked; there were some people in our ranks who sincerely felt that, in retaliation, all the students of Birmingham should stay out of school and that demonstrations should be resumed.

I was out of the city at the time, but I rushed back to Birmingham to persuade the leaders that we must not fall into the trap. We decided to take the issue into the courts and did so, through the auspices of the N.A.A.C.P. Legal Defense and Educational Fund. On May 22, the local federal district judge upheld the Birmingham Board of Education. But that same day, Judge Elbert P. Tuttle, of the Fifth Circuit Court of Appeals, not only reversed the decision of the district judge but strongly condemned the Board of Education for its action. In a time when the nation is trying to solve the problem of school drop-outs, Judge Tuttle's ruling indicated, it is an act of irresponsibility to drive those youngsters from school in retaliation for having engaged in legally permissible action to achieve their constitutional rights. The night this ruling was handed down, we had a great mass meeting. It was a jubilant moment, another victory in the titanic struggle.

The following day, in an appropriate postscript, the Alabama Supreme Court ruled Eugene "Bull" Connor and his fellow commissioners out of office, once and for all.

IV

I could not close an account of events in Birmingham without noting the tremendous moral and financial support which poured in upon us from all over the world during the six weeks of demonstrations and in the weeks and months to follow. Although we were so preoccupied with the day-to-day crises of the campaign that we did not have time to send out a formal plea for funds, letters of encouragement and donations ranging from pennies taken from piggy banks to checks of impressive size flowed into our besieged command post at the Gaston Motel and our Atlanta headquarters.

One of the most gratifying developments was the unprecedented show of unity that was displayed by the national Negro community in support of our crusade. From all over the country came Negro ministers, civil-rights leaders, entertainers, star athletes and ordinary citizens, ready to speak at our meetings or join us in jail. The N.A.A.C.P. Legal Defense and Educational Fund came to our aid several times both with money and with resourceful legal talent. Many other organizations and individuals contributed invaluable gifts of time, money and moral support.

The signing of the agreement was the climax of a long struggle for justice, freedom and human dignity. The millennium still had not come, but Birmingham had made a fresh, bold step toward equality. Today Birmingham is by no means miraculously desegregated. There is still resistance and violence. The last-ditch struggle of a segregationist governor still soils the pages of current events and it is still necessary for a harried president to invoke his highest powers so that a Negro child may go to school with a white child in Birmingham. But these factors only serve to emphasize the truth that even the segregationists know: The system to which they have been committed lies on its deathbed. The only imponderable is the question of how costly they will make the funeral.

I like to believe that Birmingham will one day become a model in southern race relations. I like to believe that the negative extremes of Birmingham's past will resolve into the positive and Utopian extreme of her future; that the sins of a dark yesterday will be redeemed in the achievements of a bright tomorrow. I have this hope because, once on a summer day, a dream came true. The city of Birmingham discovered a conscience.

VII

The Summer of Our Discontent

More than twenty-five years ago, one of the southern states adopted a new method of capital punishment. Poison gas supplanted the gallows. In its earliest stages, a microphone was placed inside the sealed death chamber so that scientific observers might hear the words of the dying prisoner to judge how the human reacted in this novel situation.

The first victim was a young Negro. As the pellet dropped into the container, and the gas curled upward, through the microphone came these words: "Save me, Joe Louis. Save me, Joe Louis. Save me, Joe Louis. . . ."

It is heartbreaking enough to ponder the last words of any person dying by force. It is even more poignant to contemplate the words of this boy because they reveal the helplessness, the loneliness and the profound despair of Negroes in that period. The condemned young Negro, groping for someone who might care for him, and had power enough to rescue him, found only the heavyweight boxing champion of the world. Joe Louis would care because he was a Negro. Joe Louis could do something because he was a fighter. In a few words the dying man had written a social commentary. Not God, not government, not charitably minded white men, but a Negro who was the world's most expert fighter, in this last extremity, was the last hope.

Less than three decades later, Negroes have discovered the fighting spirit, and the power, each within himself. Voluntarily facing death in many places, they have relied upon their own united ranks for strength and protection. In the summer of 1963, the bizarre and naïve cry to Joe Louis was replaced by a mighty shout of challenge. Helplessness was replaced by confidence as hundreds of thousands of Negroes discovered that organization, together with nonviolent direct action, was explosively, powerfully and socially transforming.

As if to dramatize the change, that summer in Birmingham another Negro world heavyweight champion appeared on the turbulent scene. Floyd Patterson came to Birmingham not as a savior, but because he felt he belonged with his people. At no moment in his pugilistic career was Patterson more of a champion than the day he appeared, far from his comfortable home, to give heart to the plain people who were engaged in another kind of bruising combat.

To measure the gains of the summer by doing some social bookkeeping—to add up the thousands of integrated restaurants, hotels, parks and swimming pools; to total the new job openings; to list the towns and cities where the victory banners now float—would be to tell less than the whole story. The full dimensions of victory can be found only by comprehending the change within the minds of millions of Negroes. From the depths in which the spirit of freedom was imprisoned, an impulse for liberty burst through. The Negro became, in his own estimation, the equal of any man. In the summer of 1963, the Negroes of America wrote an emancipation proclamation to themselves. They shook off three hundred years of psychological slavery and said: "We can make ourselves free."

The old order ends, no matter what Bastilles remain, when the enslaved, within themselves, bury the psychology of servitude. This is what happened last year in the unseen chambers of millions of minds. This was the invisible but vast field of victory.

"Am I just imagining it," asked a white business executive, "or are the Negroes I see around town, walking a little straighter these days?"

"It makes you feel this way," said a Negro organizational leader. "At last, by God, at last!"

For hundreds of years the quiet sobbing of an oppressed people had been unheard by millions of white Americans—the bitterness of the Negroes' lives remote and unfelt except by a sensitive few. Suddenly last summer the silence was broken. The lament became a shout and then a roar and for months no American, white or Negro, was insulated or unaware. The stride toward freedom lengthened and accelerated into a gallop, while the whole nation looked on. White America was forced to face the ugly facts of life as the Negro thrust himself into the consciousness of the country, and dramatized his grievances on a thousand brightly lighted stages. No period in American history, save the Civil War and the Reconstruction, records such breadth and depth to the Negro's drive to alter his life. No period records so many thaws in the frozen patterns of segregation.

It would have been pleasant to relate that Birming-

ham settled down after the storm, and moved constructively to justify the hopes of the many who wished it
well. It would have been pleasant, but it would not be
true. After partial and grudging compliance with some
of the settlement terms, the twentieth-century night
riders had yet another bloodthirsty turn on the stage.
On one horror-filled September morning they blasted
the lives from four innocent girls studying in their
Sunday-school class. Police killed another child in the
streets, and hate-filled white youths climaxed the day
with a wanton murder of a Negro boy harmlessly rid-
ing his bicycle.

These were terrible deeds but they are strangely less
terrible than the response of the dominant white community. If humane people expected the local leadership
to express remorse, they were to be disappointed. If
they hoped that a sense of atonement would quicken the
pace of constructive change, the hope was destined to
die a cold death. Instead the small beginnings of good
will seemed to wither. The City Council adamantly
refused to appoint Negro policemen. The merchants
took a few steps forward within the limited terms of
the settlement, but construed it as narrowly as possible.
The city did desegregate the library, the golf course and
later the schools and public buildings, all of which were
beyond the scope of the agreement. Yet a bleakness of
spirit militated against wholehearted progress. Perhaps
the poverty of conscience of the white majority was
most clearly illustrated at the funeral of the child martyrs. No white official attended. No white faces could
be seen save for a pathetically few courageous ministers.

More than children were buried that day; honor and decency were also interred.

A few white voices spoke out boldly, but few people listened with sympathy. The speech of Charles Morgan, delivered in the aftermath of the Sunday-school bombing, was a brave indictment of collective guilt. As a result of his forthrightness, Morgan, a prominent lawyer, was forced to abandon his practice and, with his wife and family, to leave the state.

Looking away from the political leaders, Birmingham's Negroes sought from industry a sign that it would encourage meaningful action in the spirit of the May agreement. The industry leaders were not only independent and capable, but their ownership was largely located in the North. U.S. Steel does not have to fear southern hatemongers. It is an economic oligarchy of giant power not only in Birmingham, but in the nation and the world. After months, its chairman, Roger Blough, declared from New York that despite U.S. Steel's preeminence in Birmingham, it would be improper for the corporation to seek to influence community policies in race relations. "We have fulfilled our responsibility in the Birmingham area," he said. If the community had enacted unreasonable taxes, or ordinances adversely affecting production, there is no doubt that the power of U.S. Steel would have been swiftly unleashed to determine a different result. Profits were not affected by racial injustice; indeed, they were benefited. Only people were hurt, and the greatest single power in Birmingham turned its back.

At this point many observers began to charge that

Birmingham had become the Waterloo of nonviolent direct action. The question had to be faced whether white resistance was so recalcitrant that all the heroism, daring and sacrifice of Negroes had ended, in Eliot's words: "Not with a bang but a whimper."

One hundred and seventy-five years ago, ordinary New England farmers tried to hold a hill against brilliantly trained English troops. The American farmers were outgunned and outnumbered; they had no military training, and no military discipline. But they broke two British charges on sheer nerve and spirit. Finally, running out of gun powder, they were routed. The army of King George held the hill. But Bunker Hill became a shrine of the American Revolution, and in the years of the Revolution that followed, wherever the embattled colonists marched, the Battle of Bunker Hill was an inspiration for victory. The climaxing victory at Yorktown is less well remembered than the valiant stand on the heights over Boston.

At Bunker Hill the "rabble" became an army. The British won the hill, but the colonists won their self-respect and the profound respect of their enemy. In the succeeding years of the war, the British would never again attempt to take a fortified position from the Americans. The vanquished won the war on that hill—the victors lost it.

Birmingham was different only in the sense that the Negroes did not retreat, and they won some significant gains. The desegregation of lunch counters, libraries, schools on a token basis may seem a small breach in the enormous fortress of injustice, but considering the strength of the fortress, it was a towering achievement. And Birmingham did more than this. It was a fuse—it detonated a revolution that went on to win scores of other victories.

There is a lull in Birmingham at this writing. My preference would have been to resume demonstrations in the wake of the September bombings, and I strongly urged militant action without delay. But some of those in our movement held other views. Against the formidable adversaries we faced, the fullest unity was indispensable, and I yielded. The Birmingham power structure still has an opportunity to fulfill its promises voluntarily. Whether it will act willingly, or only after renewed demonstrations, is for white Birmingham to determine. That it will finally have to act is as certain as the fact that Bunker Hill is today part of the United States of America.

II

There had been no general staff of the Revolution, and no national plan of operations. There could be no reliable records to compute the gains. Yet no one could doubt that as the Negro left 1963 behind he had taken the longest and fastest leap forward in a century.

No revolution is executed like a ballet. Its steps and gestures are not neatly designed and precisely performed. In our movement the spontaneity of its pattern was particularly in evidence. Injustice, discrimination and humiliation stood on every street corner, in every town, North and South. The selection of target cities was random. Wherever there was creative Negro leadership, wherever the white power structure responded clumsily and arrogantly, there a new storm center whirled into being.

Some cities embroiled in the conflict were by no means the worst offenders. Savannah, Atlanta, Nashville were well in advance of other southern communities, but they were not spared. The experienced Negro leadership simply determined to take a longer step forward in these localities. In a host of other communities the protests represented only the beginning, and by the time the demonstrations had ended, only a partial victory had been won. Yet for these cities the beginning was a long and satisfactory distance from nothing.

But in some places the white power structure had frozen into position. Injustice was not an evil to be corrected even partially—it was an institution to be defended. Against the nonviolent army the segregationists marshaled their legions of hatred. America's shame acquired new place names: Oxford, Mississippi—mobs shrieking for blood attack federal marshals and before order is restored two men are dead. Jackson, Mississippi—Medgar Evers, courageous N.A.A.C.P. secretary, is assassinated from ambush. Gadsden, Alabama—a new and barbarous weapon is introduced for use against Negroes, the electric cattle prod. Danville, Virginia—upright white citizens, concerned that police brutality is insufficient to intimidate Negroes, begin wearing guns in their belts.

Cambridge, Maryland, and Rome, Georgia, differed from one another in degrees of bitterness and brutality, but not in attitudes of resistance. From one perspective these engagements were all defeats for the movement. Yet from another viewpoint there were intangible elements of victory. Despite the worst these communities could inflict, they could not drive the Negroes apart. Their blows only served to unite our ranks, stiffen our resistance and tap our deepest resources of courage.

Seen in perspective, the summer of 1963 was historic partly because it witnessed the first offensive in history launched by Negroes along a broad front. The heroic but spasmodic and isolated slave revolts of the antebellum South had fused, more than a century later, into a simultaneous, massive assault against segregation. And the virtues so long regarded as the exclusive property of the white South—gallantry, loyalty and pride—had passed to the Negro demonstrators in the heat of the summer's battles.

In assessing the summer's events, some observers have tended to diminish the achievement by treating the demonstrations as an end in themselves. The heroism of the marching, the drama of the confrontation, became in their minds the total accomplishment. It is true that these elements have meaning, but to ignore the concrete and specific gains in dismantling the structure of segregation is like noticing the beauty of the rain, but failing to see that it has enriched the soil. A social movement that only moves people is merely a revolt. A movement that changes both people and institutions is a revolution.

The summer of 1963 was a revolution because it changed the face of America. Freedom was contagious. Its fever boiled in nearly one thousand cities, and by the time it had passed its peak, many thousands of lunch counters, hotels, parks and other places of public accommodation had become integrated.

Slowly and unevenly, job opportunities opened up for Negroes, though these were still more impressive in their promise than in their immediate numbers. In the larger northern cities, a more significant change in employment patterns took shape. Many firms found themselves under fire, not because they employed Negroes, but because they did not. Accustomed to ignoring the question, they were forced by its sudden overwhelming presence into a hasty search for absolving tokens. A well-trained Negro found himself sought out by industry for the first time. Many Negroes were understandably cynical as the door to opportunity was flung open to them as if they were but recent arrivals on the planet. Nevertheless, though the motives were mixed, the Negro could celebrate the slow retreat of discrimination on yet another front.

The sound of the explosion in Birmingham reached all the way to Washington, where the administration, which had firmly declared that civil-rights legislation would have to be shelved for 1963, hastily reorganized its priorities and placed a strong civil-rights bill at the top of the Congressional calendar. The task of turning the bill into law still lies ahead as I write, and the task of conforming custom to law must follow. But the surest guarantee that both will be achieved in the end is found in the massive alliance for civil rights that was formed in the summer of 1963.

III

With initial success, every social revolution simultaneously does two things: It attracts to itself fresh forces and strength, and at the same time it crystallizes the opposition. This Revolution conformed to the pattern. The positive growth of the movement was spectacular. Sympathy and support from white and Negro sources accelerated in geometric proportions. The number of S.C.L.C. affiliates jumped from 85 to 110. Conservatively estimated, more than one million Americans attended solidarity demonstrations in Washington, D.C., New York, Los Angeles, San Francisco, Cleveland, Chicago and Detroit, to mention but a few. Equally significant, though less direct in expression, hundreds of national civic, religious, labor and professional organizations speaking for tens of millions went on record in resolutions of sympathy with the unfolding movement. Because such resolutions had for so long been merely lofty expressions of empty eloquence, embattled Negroes might justifiably have deprecated their value. However, a new quality enriched these recent declarations and gave them dynamic meaning. Recognizing that the movement was now dominantly one of direct nonviolent action, for the first time they specifically called upon their supporters to join the demonstrators on the line of active struggle. This was commitment, not comment.

Sheriffs and police officers found themselves grappling with an utterly novel situation. Nationally renowned religious leaders were taking their place in jail cells along with the ordinary Negro. Sitting in the patrol wagon between the Negro domestic and the truck driver was the erect figure of the national head of the Presbyterian Church. Catholic priests and rabbis of Jewish congregations took their place on the front lines as the Old and New Testament ethic of social justice flamed with the fire that once before had transformed a world.

The crystallized opposition of the segregationists was not unexpected; but we had only dimly foreseen the resistance that came from another quarter. Victor Hugo has spoken of the "madmen of moderation" who are "unpaving hell." The descendants of Hugo's moderates appeared in the fall of 1963, bearing banners inscribed with the message: Order Before Justice.

For the most part, these moderates counted themselves as friends of the civil-rights movement; certainly they were in no sense moral bedfellows of the forces of segregation and violence. But they were now wrestling with a logic that an earlier, more passive, movement had never forced them to question. They had long settled on a simple compromise, one easy to accept and to live with. They could countenance token changes, and they had always believed these would make the Negro content. They were not asking him to stay in his old ghetto. They were ready to build a brand-new ghetto for him with a small exit door for a few. But the breath of the new movement chilled them. The Negro was insisting upon the mass application of equality to jobs, housing, education and social mobility: He sought a full life for a whole people. These moderates had come some distance in step with the thundering drums, but at the point of mass application they wanted the bugle to sound a retreat.

Resentment, impatience with militancy, and aloofness began to overcome the earlier enthusiasm. It would be easy merely to denounce this mood or ignore it, but it would be the greater wisdom to understand it. These men and women, despite their hesitations, are not our main enemies. They are our temporary obstacles and potential allies.

They are evidence that the Revolution is now ripping into roots. For too long the depth of racism in American life has been underestimated. The surgery to extract it is necessarily complex and detailed. As a beginning it is important to X-ray our history and reveal the full extent of the disease. The strands of prejudice toward Negroes are tightly wound around the American character. The prejudice has been nourished by the doctrine of race inferiority. Yet to focus upon the Negro alone as the "inferior race" of American myth is to miss the broader dimensions of the evil.

Our nation was born in genocide when it embraced the doctrine that the original American, the Indian, was an inferior race. Even before there were large numbers of Negroes on our shores, the scar of racial hatred had already disfigured colonial society. From the sixteenth century forward, blood flowed in battles over racial supremacy. We are perhaps the only nation which tried as a matter of national policy to wipe out its indigenous population. Moreover, we elevated that tragic experience into a noble crusade. Indeed, even today we have not permitted ourselves to reject or to feel remorse for this shameful episode. Our literature, our films, our drama, our folklore all exalt it.

Our children are still taught to respect the violence which reduced a red-skinned people of an earlier culture into a few fragmented groups herded into impoverished reservations. This is in sharp contrast to many nations south of the border, which assimilated their Indians, respected their culture, and elevated many of them to high position.

It was upon this massive base of racism that the prejudice toward the nonwhite was readily built, and found rapid growth. This long-standing racist ideology has corrupted and diminished our democratic ideals. It is this tangled web of prejudice from which many Americans now seek to liberate themselves, without realizing how deeply it has been woven into their consciousness.

The roots are deep, and this condition in turn influences the character of the Negro Revolution. Our history teaches us that wielding the sword against racial superiority is not effective. The bravery of the Indian, employing spears and arrows against the Winchester and the Colt, had ultimately to eventuate in defeat. On the other hand, history also teaches that submission produces no acceptable result. Nonresistance merely reinforces the myth that one race is inherently inferior to another. Negroes today are neither exercising violence nor accepting domination. They are disturbing the tranquillity of the nation until the existence of injustice is recognized as a virulent disease menacing the whole society, and is cured. The Negro's method of nonviolent direct action is not only suitable as a remedy for injustice; its very nature is such that it challenges the myth of inferiority. Even the most reluctant are forced to recognize that no inferior people could choose and successfully pursue a course involving such extensive sacrifice, bravery and skill.

We Americans have long aspired to the glories of freedom while we compromised with prejudice and servitude. Today the Negro is fighting for a finer America, and he will inevitably win the majority of the nation to his side because our hard-won heritage of freedom is ultimately more powerful than our traditions of cruelty and injustice.

To those who argue that Negroes are becoming too aggressive, and that their methods are alienating the dominant white population, there is a convincing answer. It was revealed in the survey conducted by *Newsweek* during the latter part of the summer of 1963. The surveyors interviewed a cross section of whites in depth. The striking result disclosed that overwhelming majorities favored laws to guarantee Negroes voting rights, job opportunities, good housing and integrated travel facilities. These majorities were found in the South as well as the North. Moreover, on the questions of integrated schools and restaurants, the same heavy majorities appeared in the North and the vote fell only barely short of a majority in the South.

The significant conclusion emerges that those whites without a vested interest in segregation have found acceptable exactly the changes that the nonviolent demonstrations present as their central demands. Those objectives Negroes have dramatized, fought for and defined have clearly become fair and reasonable demands to the white population, both North and

South. The summer of our discontent, far from alienating America's white citizens, brought them closer into harmony with its Negro citizens than ever before.

IV

The thundering events of the summer required an appropriate climax. The dean of Negro leaders, A. Philip Randolph, whose gifts of imagination and tireless militancy had for decades dramatized the civil-rights struggle, once again provided the uniquely suitable answer. He proposed a March on Washington to unite in one luminous action all of the forces along the far-flung front.

It took daring and boldness to embrace the idea. The Negro community was firmly united in demanding a redress of grievances, but it was divided on tactics. It had demonstrated its ability to organize skillfully in single communities, but there was no precedent for a convocation of national scope and gargantuan size. Complicating the situation were innumerable prophets of doom who feared that the slightest incidence of violence would alienate Congress and destroy all hope of legislation. Even without disturbances, they were afraid that inadequate support by Negroes would reveal weaknesses that were better concealed.

The debate on the proposal neatly polarized positions. Those with faith in the Negro's abilities, endurance and discipline welcomed the challenge. On the other side were the timid, confused and uncertain friends, along with those who had never believed in the Negro's capacity to organize anything of significance.

The conclusion was never really in doubt, because the powerful momentum of the revolutionary summer had swept aside all opposition.

Washington is a city of spectacles. Every four years, imposing presidential inaugurations attract the great and the mighty. Kings, prime ministers, heroes and celebrities of every description have been feted there for more than 150 years. But in its entire glittering history, Washington had never seen a spectacle of the size and grandeur that assembled there on August 28, 1963. Among the nearly 250,000 people who journeyed that day to the capital, there were many dignitaries and many celebrities, but the stirring emotion came from the mass of ordinary people who stood in majestic dignity as witnesses to their single-minded determination to achieve democracy in their time.

They came from almost every state in the union; they came in every form of transportation; they gave up from one to three days' pay plus the cost of transportation, which for many was a heavy financial sacrifice. They were good-humored and relaxed, yet disciplined and thoughtful. They applauded their leaders generously, but the leaders, in their own hearts, applauded their audience. Many a Negro speaker that day had his respect for his own people deepened as he felt the strength of their dedication. The enormous multitude was the living, beating heart of an infinitely noble movement. It was an army without guns, but not without strength. It was an army into which no one had to be drafted. It was white and Negro, and of all ages. It had adherents of every faith, members of every class, every profession, every political party, united by a single ideal. It was a fighting army, but no one could mistake that its most powerful weapon was love.

One significant element of the March was the participation of the white churches. Never before had they been so fully, so enthusiastically, so directly involved. One writer observed that the March "brought the country's three major religious faiths closer than any other issue in the nation's peacetime history." It was officially endorsed by the National Council of the Churches of Christ in the U.S.A., the American Baptist Convention, the Brethren Church, the United Presbyterian Church in the U.S.A., and by thousands of congregations and ministers of the Lutheran and Methodist Churches. In the Archdiocese of New York, letters were read in 402 parishes quoting Cardinal Spellman's call for accelerated activity on racial justice, with an additional appeal from the Auxiliary Bishop and Vicar General of the Archdiocese, the Most Reverend John J. Maguire. In Boston, Cardinal Gushing named eleven priests as representatives to the occasion. In addition to the American Jewish Congress, whose president, Dr. Joachim Prinz, was one of the day's chairmen, virtually every major Jewish organization, religious and secular, endorsed the March and was heavily represented at the gathering.

In unhappy contrast, the National Council of the AFL-CIO declined to support the March and adopted a position of neutrality. A number of international unions, however, independently declared their support, and were present in substantial numbers. In addition, hundreds of local unions threw their full weight into the effort.

If anyone had questioned how deeply the summer's activities had penetrated the consciousness of white America, the answer was evident in the treatment accorded the March on Washington by all the media of communication. Normally Negro activities are the object of attention in the press only when they are likely to lead to some dramatic outbreak, or possess some bizarre quality. The March was the first organized Negro operation which was accorded respect and coverage commensurate with its importance. The millions who viewed it on television were seeing an event historic not only because of the subject, but because it was being brought into their homes.

Millions of white Americans, for the first time, had a clear, long look at Negroes engaged in a serious occupation. For the first time millions listened to the informed and thoughtful words of Negro spokesmen, from all walks of life. The stereotype of the Negro suffered a heavy blow. This was evident in some of the comment, which reflected surprise at the dignity, the organization and even the wearing apparel and friendly spirit of the participants. If the press had expected something akin to a minstrel show, or a brawl, or a comic display of odd clothes and bad manners, they were disappointed. A great deal has been said about a dialogue between Negro and white. Genuinely to achieve it requires that all the media of communication open their channels wide as they did on that radiant August day.

As television beamed the image of this extraordinary gathering across the border oceans, everyone who believed in man's capacity to better himself had a moment of inspiration and confidence in the future of the human race. And every dedicated American could be proud that a dynamic experience of democracy in his nation's capital had been made visible to the world.

VIII

The Days to Come

One hundred and fifty years ago, when the Negro was a thing, a chattel whose body belonged to his white master, there were certain slaveowners who worked out arrangements whereby a slave could purchase himself, and become a "freedman." An enterprising young man who became enamored of a slave sweetheart worked desperately—in what time he could find away from his labors—and, over a period of years, amassed sufficient capital to earn his own liberation and that of his betrothed. Many a Negro mother, after toiling from dawn until sundown, would spend the remainder of the night washing clothes and putting away the pennies and nickels so earned until, with the passage of years, a few hundred dollars had been accumulated. Often she struggled and sacrificed to purchase not her own freedom but that of a son or daughter. The hard-earned dollars were paid to the slaveowner in exchange for a legal instrument of manumission which declared its holder relieved of the bondage of physical slavery.

As this movement grew, some Negroes devoted their lives to the purchase and liberation of others. A servant of Thomas Jefferson worked for some forty years and earned ten thousand dollars, with which she was able to obtain the liberation of nineteen fellow humans. Still later, a few dedicated and humanitarian white men took a crusade to the public for funds to ransom black people from the degradation which their abductors had imposed upon them. Even James Russell Lowell, who was opposed to compensated emancipation, wrote to a friend: "If a man comes and asks us to help him buy his wife or his child, what are we to do?"

"Help me buy my mother," or "Help me buy my child," was a poignant appeal. It brought the deep torture of black people's souls into stark and shocking focus for many whites to whom the horror of slavery had been emotionally remote.

As one approaches the emancipation of today's Negro from all those traumatic ties that still bind him to slaveries other than the physical, this shadowed footnote, this half-forgotten history of a system that bartered dignity for dollars, stands as a painful reminder of the capacity of society to remain complacent in the midst of injustice. Today's average American may well shudder to think that such tawdry transactions were acceptable to his grandparents' parents. Yet that same American may not realize that callous indifference to human suffering exists to this day, when people who consider themselves men of good will are still asking: "What is the Negro willing to pay if we give him his freedom?"

This is not to say that today's society wants dollars and cents in order to grant the Negro his rights. But there is a terrible parallel between the outstretched and greedy hand of a slave trafficker who sold a Negro his own person, and the uplifted and admonishing finger of people who say today: "What more will the Negro expect if he gains such rights as integrated schools, public facilities, voting rights and progress in housing? Will he, like Oliver Twist, demand more?"

What is implied here is the amazing assumption that society has the right to bargain with the Negro for the freedom which inherently belongs to him. Some of the most vocal liberals believe they have a valid basis for demanding that, in order to gain certain rights, the Negro ought to pay for them out of the funds of patience and passivity which he has stored up for so many years. What these people do not realize is that gradualism and moderation are not the answer to the great moral indictment which, in the Revolution of 1963, finally came to stand in the center of our national stage. What they do not realize is that it is no more possible to be half free than it is to be half alive.

In a sense, the well-meaning or the ill-meaning American who asks: "What more will the Negro want?" or "When will he be satisfied?" or "What will it take to make these demonstrations cease?" is asking the Negro to purchase something that already belongs to him by every concept of law, justice and our Judaeo-Christian heritage. Moreover, he is asking the Negro to accept half the loaf and to pay for that half by waiting willingly for the other half to be distributed in crumbs over a hard and protracted winter of injustice. I would like to ask those people who seek to apportion to us the rights they have always enjoyed whether they believe that the framers of the Declaration of Independence intended that liberty should be divided into installments, doled out on a deferred-payment plan. Did not nature create birth as a single process? Is not freedom the negation of servitude? Does not one have to end totally for the other to begin?

It is because the Negro knows that no person—as well as no nation—can truly exist half slave and half free that he has embroidered upon his banners the significant word NOW. The Negro is saying that the time has come for our nation to take that firm stride into freedom—not simply toward freedom—which will pay a long-overdue debt to its citizens of color. Centuries ago, civilization acquired the certain knowledge that man had emerged from barbarity only to the degree that he recognized his relatedness to his fellow man. Civilization, particularly in the United States, has long possessed the material wealth and resources to feed, clothe and shelter all of its citizens. Civilization has endowed man with the capacity to organize change, to conceive and implement plans. It is ironic that, for so many years, the armed forces of this nation, even in time of war, were prisoners of the southern system of segregation. The military establishment could tear a man away from his wife and child, and reorient, within weeks, his entire mode of life and conduct. But not until World War II did the Army begin to conceive that it had the right, the obligation and the ability to say that a white man in uniform must respect the dignity of a black man in uniform.

We need a powerful sense of determination to banish the ugly blemish of racism scarring the image of America. We can, of course, try to temporize, negotiate small, inadequate changes and prolong the timetable of freedom in the hope that the narcotics of delay will dull the pain of progress. We can try, but we shall certainly fail. The shape of the world will not permit us the luxury of gradualism and procrastination. Not only is it immoral, it will not work. It will not work because Negroes know they have the right to be free. It will not work because Negroes have discovered, in nonviolent direct action, an irresistible force to propel what has been for so long an immovable object. It will not work because it retards the progress not only of the Negro, but of the nation as a whole.

As certain as it is that a planned gradualism will not work, neither will unplanned spontaneity. When the locomotive of history roared through the nineteenth century and the first half of the twentieth, it left the nation's black masses standing forlornly at dismal terminals. They were unschooled, untrained, ill-housed, and ill-fed. The scientific achievements of today, particularly the explosive advance of automation, may be blessings to our economy, but for the Negro they are a curse. Years back, the Negro could boast that 350,000 of his race were employed by the railroads. Today, less than 50,000 work in this area of transportation. This is but a symbol of what has happened in the coal mines, the steel mills, the packing houses, in all industries that once employed large numbers of Negroes. The livelihood of millions has dwindled down to a frightening fraction because the unskilled and semiskilled jobs they filled have disappeared under the magic of automation. In that separate culture of poverty in which the half-educated Negro lives, an economic depression rages today. To deal with this disaster by opening some doors

to all, and all doors to some, amounts merely to organizing chaos.

What is true in the field of employment also ap-
plies to housing. We cannot tap the ghettos in order to
screen out a few representative individuals, leaving others to wait in grim shacks and tenements. Nor can the
vast ghettos of many cities be turned inside out in one
convulsive gesture, spilling people of all varieties into
one torrent to flow wherever the social gravity pulls.
Either of these courses—gradualism or directionless
spontaneity—would generate social turmoil both for
the deprived and for the privileged.

Solutions to the complex plight of the Negro will
not be easy. This does not signify that they are impossible. Recognizing these complexities as challenges
rather than as obstacles, we will make progress if we
freely admit that we have no magic. We will make
progress if we accept the fact that four hundred years
of sinning cannot be canceled out in four minutes of
atonement. Neither can we allow the guilty to tailor
their atonement in such a manner as to visit another
four seconds of deliberate hurt upon the victim.

II

Recently, Roy Wilkins and I appeared on the television program *Meet the Press*. There were the usual questions about how much more the Negro wants, but
there seemed to be a new undercurrent of implications
related to the sturdy new strength of our movement.
Without the courtly complexities, we were, in effect,
being asked if we could be trusted to hold back the
surging tides of discontent so that those on the shore

would not be made too uncomfortable by the buffeting and onrushing waves. Some of the questions implied that our leadership would be judged in accordance with our capacity to "keep the Negro from going too far." The quotes are mine, but I think the phrase mirrors the thinking of the panelists as well as of many other white Americans.

The show did not permit time for an adequate answer to the implications behind the question: "What more does the Negro want?" When we say that the Negro wants absolute and immediate freedom and equality, not in Africa or in some imaginary state, but right here in this land today, the answer is disturbingly terse to people who are not certain they wish to believe it. Yet this is the fact. Negroes no longer are tolerant of or interested in compromise. American history is replete with compromise. As splendid as are the words of the Declaration of Independence, there are disquieting implications in the fact that the original phrasing was altered to delete a condemnation of the British monarch for his espousal of slavery. American history chronicles the Missouri Compromise, which permitted the spread of slavery to new states; the Hayes-Tilden Compromise, which withdrew the federal troops from the South and signaled the end of Reconstruction; the Supreme Court's compromise in *Plessy v. Ferguson*, which enunciated the infamous "separate but equal" philosophy. These measures compromised not only the liberty of the Negro but the integrity of America. In the bursting mood that has overtaken the Negro in 1963, the word "compromise" is profane and pernicious. The majority of Negro leadership is innately opposed to compromise. Even were this not true, no Negro leader today could divert the direction of the movement or its compelling and inspired forward motion.

Many of our white brothers misunderstand this fact because many of them fail to interpret correctly the nature of the Negro Revolution. Some believe that it is the work of skilled agitators who have the power to raise or lower the floodgates at will. Such a movement, maneuverable by a talented few, would not be a genuine revolution. This Revolution is genuine because it was born from the same womb that always gives birth to massive social upheavals—the womb of intolerable conditions and unendurable situations. In this time and circumstance, no leader or set of leaders could have acted as ringmasters, whipping a whole race out of purring contentment into leonine courage and action. If such credit is to be given to any single group, it might well go to the segregationists, who, with their callous and cynical code, helped to arouse and ignite the righteous wrath of the Negro. In this connection, I am reminded of something President Kennedy said to me at the White House following the signing of the Birmingham agreement.

"Our judgment of Bull Connor should not be too harsh," he commented. "After all, in his way, he has done a good deal for civil-rights legislation this year."

It was the people who moved their leaders, not the leaders who moved the people. Of course, there were generals, as there must be in every army. But the command post was in the bursting hearts of millions of Negroes. When such a people begin to move, they create their own theories, shape their own destinies, and choose the leaders who share their own philosophy. A leader who understands this kind of mandate knows that he must be sensitive to the anger, the impatience, the frustration, the resolution that have been loosed in his people. Any leader who tries to bottle up these emotions is sure to be blown asunder in the ensuing explosion.

A number of commentators have implied that a band of militants has seized the offensive and that the "sound and sensible" leaders are being drawn into action unwillingly in order to keep control from being wrested out of their hands. Certainly there are, and will continue to be, differences of opinion among Negro leaders, differences relating to certain specific, tactical moves; but to describe the meaning of recent events as the seizure of control by a few who have driven out the rest exaggerates the importance of the differences. The enemies of racial progress—and even some of its "friends," who are "for it, but not so fast"—would delight in believing that there is chaos up front in the civil-rights ranks.

The hard truth is that the unity of the movement is a remarkable feature of major importance. The fact that different organizations place varying degrees of emphasis on certain tactical approaches is not indicative of disunity. Unity has never meant uniformity. If it had, it would not have been possible for such dedicated democrats as Thomas Jefferson and George Washington, a radical such as Thomas Paine and an autocrat such as Alexander Hamilton to lead a unified American Revolution. Jefferson, Washington, Paine and Hamilton could collaborate because the urge of the colonials to be free had matured into a powerful mandate. This is what has happened to the determination of the Negro to liberate himself. When the cry for justice has hardened into a palpable force, it becomes irresistible. This is a truth which wise leadership and a sensible society ultimately come to realize.

In the current struggle, there is one positive course of action. There is no alternative, for the alternative would connote a rear march, and the Negro, far from being willing to retrogress, is not even willing to mark time. In this Revolution no plans have been written for retreat. Those who will not get into step will find that the parade has passed them by.

Someone once wrote: "When you are right, you cannot be too radical; when you are wrong, you cannot be too conservative." The Negro knows he is right. He has not organized for conquest or to gain spoils or to enslave those who have injured him. His goal is not to capture that which belongs to someone else. He merely wants and will have what is honorably his. When these long-withheld rights and privileges are looked upon as prizes he seeks from impertinent greed, only one answer can come from the depths of a Negro's being. That answer can be summarized in the hallowed American words: "If this be treason, make the most of it."

The sooner our society admits that the Negro Revolution is no momentary outburst soon to subside into placid passivity, the easier the future will be for us all.

III

Among the many vital jobs to be done, the nation must not only radically readjust its attitude toward the Negro in the compelling present, but must incorporate in its planning some compensatory consideration for the handicaps he has inherited from the past. It is impossible to create a formula for the future which does not take into account that our society has been doing something special *against* the Negro for hundreds of years. How then can he be absorbed into the mainstream of American life if we do not do something special *for* him now, in order to balance the equation and equip him to compete on a just and equal basis?

Whenever this issue of compensatory or preferential treatment for the Negro is raised, some of our friends recoil in horror. The Negro should be granted equality, they agree; but he should ask nothing more. On the surface, this appears reasonable, but it is not realistic. For it is obvious that if a man is entered at the starting line in a race three hundred years after another man, the first would have to perform some impossible feat in order to catch up with his fellow runner.

Several years ago, Prime Minister Nehru was telling me how his nation is handling the difficult problem of the untouchables, a problem not unrelated to the American Negro dilemma. The prime minister admitted that many Indians still harbor a prejudice against these long-oppressed people, but that it has become unpopular to exhibit this prejudice in any form. In part, this change in climate was created through the moral leadership of the late Mahatma Gandhi, who set an example for the nation by adopting an untouchable as his daughter. In part, it is the result of the Indian Constitution, which specifies that discrimination against the untouchables is a crime, punishable by imprisonment.

The Indian government spends millions of rupees annually developing housing and job opportunities in villages heavily inhabited by untouchables. Moreover, the prime minister said, if two applicants compete for entrance into a college or university, one of the applicants being an untouchable and the other of high caste, the school is required to accept the untouchable.

Professor Lawrence Reddick, who was with me during the interview, asked: "But isn't that discrimination?"

"Well, it may be," the prime minister answered. "But this is our way of atoning for the centuries of injustices we have inflicted upon these people."

America must seek its own ways of atoning for the injustices she has inflicted upon her Negro citizens. I do not suggest atonement for atonement's sake or because there is need for self-punishment. I suggest atonement as the moral and practical way to bring the Negro's standards up to a realistic level.

In facing the new American dilemma, the relevant question is not: "What more does the Negro want?" but rather: "How can we make freedom real and substantial for our colored citizens? What just course will ensure the greatest speed and completeness? And how do we combat opposition and overcome obstacles arising from the defaults of the past?"

New ways are needed to handle the issue because we have come to a new stage in the development of our nation and of one in ten of its people. The surging power of the Negro revolt and the genuineness of good will that has come from many white Americans indicate that the time is ripe for broader thinking and action.

The Negro today is not struggling for some abstract, vague rights, but for concrete and prompt improvement in his way of life. What will it profit him to be able to send his children to an integrated school if the family income is insufficient to buy them school clothes? What will he gain by being permitted to move to an integrated neighborhood if he cannot afford to do so because he is unemployed or has a low-paying job with no future? During the lunch-counter sit-ins in Greensboro, North Carolina, a nightclub comic observed that, had the demonstrators been served, some of them could not have paid for the meal. Of what advantage is it to the Negro to establish that he can be served in integrated restaurants, or accommodated in integrated hotels, if he is bound to the kind of financial servitude which will not allow him to take a vacation or even to take his wife out to dine? Negroes must not only have the right to go into any establishment open to the public, but they must also be absorbed into our economic system in such a manner that they can afford to exercise that right.

The struggle for rights is, at bottom, a struggle for opportunities. In asking for something special, the Negro is not seeking charity. He does not want to languish on welfare rolls any more than the next man. He does not want to be given a job he cannot handle. Neither, however, does he want to be told that there is no place where he can be trained to handle it. So with equal opportunity must come the practical, realistic aid which will equip him to seize it. Giving a pair of shoes to a man who has not learned to walk is a cruel jest.

Special measures for the deprived have always been accepted in principle by the United States. The National Urban League, in an excellent statement, has underlined the fact that we find nothing strange about the Marshall Plan and technical assistance to handicapped peoples around the world, and suggested that we can do no less for our own handicapped multitudes. Throughout history we have adhered to this principle. It was the principle behind land grants to farmers who fought in the Revolutionary Army. It was inherent in the establishment of child labor laws, social security, unemployment compensation, manpower retraining programs and countless other measures that the nation accepted as logical and moral.

During World War II, our fighting men were deprived of certain advantages and opportunities. To make up for this, they were given a package of veterans rights, significantly called a "Bill of Rights." The major features of this GI Bill of Rights included subsidies for trade school or college education, with living expenses provided during the period of study. Veterans were given special concessions enabling them to buy homes without cash, with lower interest rates and easier repayment terms. They could negotiate loans from banks to launch businesses, using the government as an endorser of any losses. They received special points to place them ahead in competition for civil-service jobs. They were provided with medical care and long-term financial grants if their physical condition had been impaired by their military service. In addition to these legally granted rights, a strong social climate for many years favored the preferential employment of veterans in all walks of life.

In this way, the nation was compensating the veteran for his time lost, in school or in his career or in business. Such compensatory treatment was approved by the majority of Americans. Certainly the Negro has been deprived. Few people consider the fact that, in addition to being enslaved for two centuries, the Negro was, during all those years, robbed of the wages of his toil. No amount of gold could provide an adequate compensation for the exploitation and humiliation of the Negro in America down through the centuries. Not all the wealth of this affluent society could meet the bill. Yet a price can be placed on unpaid wages. The ancient common law has always provided a remedy for the appropriation of the labor of one human being by another. This law should be made to apply for American Negroes. The payment should be in the form of a massive program by the government of special, compensatory measures which could be regarded as a settlement in accordance with the accepted practice of common law. Such measures would certainly be less expensive than any computation based on two centuries of unpaid wages and accumulated interest.

I am proposing, therefore, that, just as we granted a GI Bill of Rights to war veterans, America launch a broad-based and gigantic Bill of Rights for the Disadvantaged, our veterans of the long siege of denial.

Such a bill could adapt almost every concession given to the returning soldier without imposing an undue burden on our economy. A Bill of Rights for the Disadvantaged would immediately transform the conditions of Negro life. The most profound alteration would not reside so much in the specific grants as in the basic psychological and motivational transformation of the Negro. I would challenge skeptics to give such a bold new approach a test for the next decade. I contend that the decline in school dropouts, family breakups, crime rates, illegitimacy, swollen relief rolls and other social evils would stagger the imagination. Change in human psychology is normally a slow process, but it is safe to predict that, when a people is ready for change as the Negro has shown himself ready today, the response is bound to be rapid and constructive.

While Negroes form the vast majority of America's disadvantaged, there are millions of white poor who would also benefit from such a bill. The moral justification for special measures for Negroes is rooted in the robberies inherent in the institution of slavery. Many poor whites, however, were the derivative victims of slavery. As long as labor was cheapened by the involuntary servitude of the black man, the freedom of white labor, especially in the South, was little more than a myth. It was free only to bargain from the depressed base imposed by slavery upon the whole labor market. Nor did this derivative bondage end when formal slavery gave way to the de facto slavery of discrimination. To this day the white poor also suffer deprivation and the humiliation of poverty if not of color. They are chained by the weight of discrimination, though its badge of degradation does not mark them. It corrupts their lives, frustrates their opportunities and withers their education. In one sense it is more evil for them, because it has confused so many by prejudice that they have supported their own oppressors.

It is a simple matter of justice that America, in dealing creatively with the task of raising the Negro from backwardness, should also be rescuing a large stratum of the forgotten white poor. A Bill of Rights for the Disadvantaged could mark the rise of a new era, in which the full resources of the society would be used to attack the tenacious poverty which so paradoxically exists in the midst of plenty.

The nation will also have to find the answer to full employment, including a more imaginative approach than has yet been conceived for neutralizing the perils of automation. Today, as the unskilled and semiskilled Negro attempts to mount the ladder of economic security, he finds himself in competition with the white working man at the very time when automation is scrapping forty thousand jobs a week. Though this is perhaps the inevitable product of social and economic upheaval, it is an intolerable situation, and Negroes will not long permit themselves to be pitted against white workers for an ever-decreasing supply of jobs. The energetic and creative expansion of work opportunities, in both the public and private sectors of our economy, is an imperative worthy of the richest nation on earth, whose abundance is an embarrassment as long as millions of poor are imprisoned and constantly self-renewed within an expanding population.

In addition to such an economic program, a social-work apparatus on a large scale is required. Whole generations have been left behind as the majority of the population advanced. These lost generations have never learned basic social skills on a functional level—the skills of reading, writing, arithmetic; of applying for jobs; of exercising the rights of citizenship, including the right to vote. Moreover, rural and urban poverty has not only stultified lives; it has created emotional disturbances, many of which find expression in anti-social acts. The most tragic victims are children, whose impoverished parents, frantically struggling day by day for food and a place to live, have been unable to create the stable home necessary for the wholesome growth of young minds.

Opportunities and the means to exploit them are, however, still inadequate to assure equality, justice and decency in our national life. There is an imperative need for legislation to outlaw our present grotesque legal mores. We find ourselves in a society where the supreme law of the land, the Constitution, is rendered inoperative in vast areas of the nation. State, municipal and county laws and practices negate constitutional mandates as blatantly as if each community were an independent medieval duchy. In the event that strong civil-rights legislation is written into the books in the session of Congress now sitting, and that a Bill of Rights for the Disadvantaged might follow, enforcement will still meet with massive resistance in many parts of the country.

In the thirties, the country was faced with a parallel challenge. Powerful and antagonistic elements all over the land were strongly resisting the efforts of workers to organize to secure a living wage and decent conditions of work. It is interesting to note that some of the states that today are opposing progress in civil rights were the same that defied the unions' efforts during the thirties. Then, as now, the task of penetrating to thousands of communities in order to ensure the rights of their citizens over the opposition of hostile interests posed a substantial and complex challenge to federal power.

The national government found a method of solving this problem. The Wagner Act was written, establishing the rights of labor to organize. Regional labor boards were appointed, armed with the power to ascertain facts, conduct elections, issue binding orders and, through the utilization of these powers, to compel compliance. Of course, the strength of a newly aroused labor movement, with a well-sharpened strike weapon, stimulated cooperation. The twofold effect of a comprehensive law, backed by a zealous government and the power of organized labor, within a few short years transformed thousands of strife-torn, antilabor citadels into orderly, unionized communities.

A law designed to operate in the fashion of the Wagner Act may well be the answer to some of the problems of civil-rights enforcement during the next decade. Recently, Senator Harrison Williams of New Jersey presented a bill to the Senate incorporating many similar proposals. Other senators searching for legislative solutions should be encouraged to consider measures along these lines.

IV

The pattern of future action must be examined not only from the standpoint of the strengths inherent in the civil-rights movement, but simultaneously from a study of the resistance we have yet to face. While we can celebrate that the civil-rights movement has come of age, we must also recognize that the basic recalcitrance of the South has not yet been broken. True, substantial progress has been made: It is deeply significant that a powerful financial and industrial force has emerged in some southern regions, which is prepared to tolerate change in order to avoid costly chaos. This group in turn permits the surfacing of middle-class elements who are further splitting the monolithic front of segregation. Southern church, labor and human-relations groups today articulate sentiments that only yesterday would have been pronounced treasonable in the region. Nevertheless, a deeply entrenched social force, convinced that it need yield nothing of substantial importance, continues to dominate southern life. And even in the North, the will to preserve the status quo maintains a rocklike hardness underneath the cosmetic surface.

In order to assure that the work of democracy so well begun in the summer of 1963 will move forward steadily in the seasons to come, the Negro freedom movement will need to secure and extend its alliances with like-minded groups in the larger community. Already, in the complex dilemma of fast-paced progress and persistent poverty, the Negro has emerged as a dissatisfied, vibrant and powerful element, armed with a method for articulating and acting out his protest. His example has not gone unobserved by others, of all races, who live in equally desperate circumstances. Inevitably, before long, a broad-based legion of the deprived, white and Negro, will coalesce and restructure an old order based too long on injustice.

In the case of organized labor, an alliance with the Negro civil-rights movement is not a matter of choice but a necessity. If Negroes have almost no rights in the South, labor has few more; if Negroes have inadequate political influence in Congress, labor is barely better off; if automation is a threat to Negroes, it is equally a menace to organized labor.

The withholding of support from the March on Washington by the National Council of the AFL-CIO was a blunder, and served to strengthen the prevalent feeling that organized labor, not only on the national level but frequently on the local level as well, is lacking today in statesmanship, vigor and modernity. This default is all the more noticeable because labor's history contains a rich record of understanding toward racial issues. When labor fought for recognition during the thirties and forties, and thus became the principal "civil-rights" issue of the time, disadvantaged Negroes joined in its bitter struggles and shared every sacrifice. Negroes battling for their own recognition today have a right to expect more from their old allies. Nothing would hold back the forces of progress in American life more effectively than a schism between the Negro and organized labor.

Another necessary alliance is with the federal government. It is the obligation of government to move resolutely to the side of the freedom movement. There is a right and a wrong side in this conflict and the government does not belong in the middle.

Without the resources of the federal government, the task of achieving practical civil rights must overwhelm voluntary organization. It is not generally realized that the burden of court decision, such as the Supreme Court decision on school desegregation, places the responsibility on the individual Negro who is compelled to bring a suit in order to obtain his rights. In effect, the most impoverished Americans, facing powerfully equipped adversaries, are required to finance and conduct complex litigation that may involve tens of thousands of dollars. To have shaped remedies in this form for existing inequities in our national life was in itself a concession to segregationists. The unsound consequences of this procedure are hampering progress to this day. A solution can only be achieved if the government assumes the responsibility for all legal proceedings, facing the reality that the poor and the unemployed already fight an unequal daily struggle to stay alive. To be forced to accumulate resources for legal actions imposes intolerable hardships on the already overburdened.

Perhaps the most determining factor in the role of the federal government is the tone set by the chief executive in his words and his actions. In the past few years, I have met and talked with three presidents, and have grown increasingly aware of the play of their temperaments on their approach to civil rights, a cause that all three have espoused in principle.

No one could discuss racial justice with President Eisenhower without coming away with mixed emotions. His personal sincerity on the issue was pronounced, and he had a magnificent capacity to communicate it to individuals. However, he had no ability to translate it to the public, or to define the problem as a supreme domestic issue. I have always felt that he failed because he knew that his colleagues and advisers did not share his views, and he had no disposition to fight even for cherished beliefs. Moreover, President Eisenhower could not be committed to anything which involved a structural change in the architecture of American society. His conservatism was fixed and rigid, and any evil defacing the nation had to be extracted bit by bit with a tweezer because the surgeon's knife was an instrument too radical to touch this best of all possible societies.

President Kennedy was a strongly contrasted personality. There were, in fact, two John Kennedys. One presided in the first two years under pressure of the uncertainty caused by his razor-thin margin of victory. He vacillated, trying to sense the direction his leadership could travel while retaining and building support for his administration. However, in 1963, a new Kennedy had emerged. He had found that public opinion was not in a rigid mold. American political thought was not committed to conservatism, nor radicalism, nor moderation. It was above all fluid. As such it contained trends rather than hard lines, and affirmative leadership could guide it into constructive channels.

President Kennedy was not given to sentimental expressions of feeling. He had, however, a deep grasp of the dynamics of and the necessity for social change. His work for international amity was a bold effort on a world scale. His last speech on race relations was the most earnest, human and profound appeal for understanding and justice that any president has uttered since the first days of the Republic. Uniting his flair for leadership with a program of social progress, he was at his death undergoing a transformation from a hesitant leader with unsure goals to a strong figure with deeply appealing objectives.

The assassination of President Kennedy killed not only a man but a complex of illusions. It demolished the myth that hate and violence can be confined in an airtight chamber to be employed against but a few. Suddenly the truth was revealed that hate is a contagion; that it grows and spreads as a disease; that no society is so healthy that it can automatically maintain its immunity. If a smallpox epidemic had been raging in the South, President Kennedy would have been urged to avoid the area. There was a plague afflicting the South, but its perils were not perceived.

Negroes tragically know political assassination well. In the life of Negro civil-rights leaders, the whine of the bullet from ambush, the roar of the bomb have all too often broken the night's silence. They have replaced lynching as a political weapon. More than a decade ago, sudden death came to Mr. and Mrs. Harry T. Moore, N.A.A.C.P. leaders in Florida. The Reverend George Lee of Belzoni, Mississippi, was shot to death on the steps of a rural courthouse. The bombings multiplied. Nineteen sixty-three was a year of assassinations. Medgar Evers in Jackson, Mississippi; William Moore in Alabama; six Negro children in Birmingham—and who could doubt that these too were political assassinations?

The unforgivable default of our society has been its failure to apprehend the assassins. It is a harsh judgment, but undeniably true, that the cause of the indifference was the identity of the victims. Nearly all were Negroes. And so the plague spread until it claimed the most eminent American, a warmly loved and respected president. The words of Jesus "Inasmuch as ye have done it unto one of the least of these my brethren, ye have done it unto me" were more than a figurative expression; they were a literal prophecy.

We were all involved in the death of John Kennedy. We tolerated hate; we tolerated the sick stimulation of violence in all walks of life; and we tolerated the differential application of law, which said that a man's life was sacred only if we agreed with his views. This may explain the cascading grief that flooded the country in late November. We mourned a man who had become the pride of the nation, but we grieved as well for ourselves because we knew we were sick.

In sadness and remorse the American people have searched for a monument big enough to honor John Kennedy. Airports, bridges, space centers and highways now bear his name. Yet the foundations for the most majestic tribute of all were laid in the days immediately following his death. Louis Harris, polling a cross section of the country for its reaction to the assassination, wrote that "the death of President Kennedy produced a profound change in the thinking of the American people; a massive rejection of extremism from either right or left, accompanied by an individual sense of guilt for not working more for tolerance toward others." If the tragically premature end of John Kennedy will prove to have so enlarged the sense of humanity of a whole people, that in itself will be a monument of enduring strength.

I had been fortunate enough to meet Lyndon Johnson during his tenure as vice president. He was not then a presidential aspirant, and was searching for his role under a man who not only had a four-year term to complete but was confidently expected to serve out yet another term as chief executive. Therefore, the essential issues were easier to reach, and were unclouded by political considerations.

His approach to the problem of civil rights was not identical with mine—nor had I expected it to be. Yet his careful practicality was nonetheless clearly no mask to conceal indifference. His emotional and intellectual involvement were genuine and devoid of adornment. It was conspicuous that he was searching for a solution to a problem he knew to be a major shortcoming in American life. I came away strengthened in my conviction that an undifferentiated approach to white southerners could be a grave error, all too easy for Negro leaders in the heat of bitterness. Later, it was Vice President Johnson I had in mind when I wrote in *The Nation* that the white South was splitting, and that progress could be furthered by driving a wedge between the rigid segregationists and the new white elements whose love of their land was stronger than the grip of old habits and customs.

Today, the dimensions of Johnson's leadership have spread from a region to a nation. His recent expressions, public and private, indicate that he has a comprehensive grasp of contemporary problems. He has seen that poverty and unemployment are grave and growing catastrophes, and he is aware that those caught most fiercely in the grip of this economic holocaust are Negroes. Therefore, he has set the twin goal of a battle against discrimination within the war against poverty.

I have no doubt that we may continue to differ concerning the tempo and the tactical design required to combat the impending crisis. But I do not doubt that the president is approaching the solution with sincerity, with realism and, thus far, with wisdom. I hope his course will be straight and true. I will do everything in my power to make it so by outspoken agreement whenever proper, and determined opposition whenever necessary.

V

For many months during the election campaign of 1960, my close friends urged me to declare my support for John Kennedy. I spent many troubled hours searching for the responsible and fair decision. I was impressed by his qualities, by many elements of his record, and by his program. I had learned to enjoy and respect his charm and his incisive mind. Beyond that I was personally obligated to him and to his brother, Robert Kennedy, for their intervention during my 1960 imprisonment in Georgia.

However, I felt that the weight of history was against a formal endorsement. No president except perhaps Lincoln had ever sufficiently given that degree of support to our struggle for freedom to justify our confidence. I had to conclude that the then known facts about Kennedy were not adequate to make an unqualified judgment in his favor. Today, I still deeply believe that the civil-rights movement must retain its independence. And yet, had President Kennedy lived, I would probably have endorsed him in the forthcoming election.

I did not arrive at this conclusion only because I

learned to repose more confidence in President Kennedy. Perhaps more basic is the fact that a new stage in civil rights has been reached, which calls for a new policy. What has changed is our strength. The upsurge of power in the civil-rights movement has given it greater maneuverability, and substantial security. It is now strong enough to form alliances, to make commitments in exchange for pledges, and if the pledges are unredeemed, it remains powerful enough to walk out without being shattered or weakened.

Negroes have traditionally positioned themselves too far from the inner arena of political decision. Few other minority groups have maintained a political aloofness and a nonpartisan posture as rigidly and as long as Negroes. The Germans, Irish, Italians, and Jews, after a period of acclimatization, moved inside political formations and exercised influence. Negroes, partly by choice but substantially by exclusion, have operated outside of the political structures, functioning instead essentially as a pressure group with limited effect.

For some time, this reticence protected the Negro from corruption and manipulation by political bosses. The cynical district leader directing his ignorant flock to vote blindly at his dictation is a relatively rare phenomenon in Negro life. The very few Negro political bosses have no gullible following. Those who give them support do so because they are persuaded that these men are their only available forthright spokesmen. By and large, Negroes remain essentially skeptical, issue-oriented, and independent-minded. Their lack of formal learning is no barrier when it comes to making intelligent choices among alternatives.

The Negroes' real problem has been that they have seldom had adequate choices. Political life, as a rule, did not attract the best elements of the Negro community, and white candidates who represented their views were few and far between. However, in avoiding the trap of domination by unworthy leaders, Negroes fell into the bog of political inactivity. They avoided victimization by any political group by withholding a significant commitment to any organization or individual.

The price they paid was reflected in the meager influence they could exercise for a positive program. But in the more recent years, as a result of their direct-action programs, their political potentiality has become manifest both to themselves and to the political leadership. An active rethinking is taking place in all Negro circles concerning their role in political life. The conclusion is already certain: It is time for Negroes to abandon abstract political neutrality and become less timid about voting alliances. If we bear in mind that alliance does not mean reliance, our independence will remain inviolate. We can and should selectively back candidates whose record justifies confidence. We can, because of our strength; we should, because those who work with us must feel we can help them concretely. Conversely, those who deny us their support should not feel that no one will get our help, but instead they must understand that when they spurn us it is likely not only that they will lose, but that their opponent will gain.

The Negro potential for political power is now sub-

stantial. Negroes are strategically situated in large cities, especially in the North but also in the South, and
these cities in turn are decisive in state elections. These
same states are the key in a presidential race, and frequently determine the nomination. This unique factor gives Negroes enormous leverage in the balance of
power. The effects of this leverage are already evident.
In South Carolina, for example, the 10,000-vote margin that gave President Kennedy his victory in 1960
was the Negro vote. Since then, some half a million
new Negro voters have been added to southern registration rolls. Today, a shift in the Negro vote could
upset the outcome of several state contests, and affect
the result of a presidential election.

Moreover, the subjective elements of political power
—persistence, aggressiveness and discipline—are also
attributes of the new movement. Political leaders are
infinitely respectful toward any group that has an abundance of energy to ring doorbells, man the street corners and escort voters to the polls. Negroes in their
demonstrations and voter-registration campaigns have
been acquiring excellent training in just these tasks.
They also have discipline perhaps beyond that of any
other group, because it has become a condition of sur-
vival. Consider the political power that would be generated if the million Americans who marched in 1963
also put their energy directly into the electoral process.

Already, in some states and cities in the South, a de
facto alliance of Negro and sympathetic white voters
has elected a new type of local official—nonintegra-
tionist, but nonsegregationist too. As Negroes extend
their energetic voting and registration campaigns, and

attain bloc-voting importance, such officials will move from dead center and slowly find the courage to stand unequivocally for integration.

On the national scene, the Congress today is dominated by southern reactionaries whose control of the key committees enables them to determine legislation. Disenfranchisement of the Negro and the nonexercise of the vote by poor whites have permitted the southern congressman to wrest his election from a tiny group, which he manipulates easily to return him again and again to office. United with northern reactionaries, these unrepresentative legislators have crippled the country by blocking urgently needed action. Only with the growth of an enlightened electorate, white and Negro together, can we put a quick end to this century-old stranglehold of a minority on the nation's legislative processes.

There are those who shudder at the idea of a political bloc, particularly a Negro bloc, which conjures up visions of racial exclusiveness. This concern is, however, unfounded. Not exclusiveness but effectiveness is the aim of bloc voting; by forming a bloc a minority makes its voice heard. The Negro minority will unite for political action for the same reason that it will seek to function in alliance with other groups—because in this way it can compel the majority to listen.

It is well to remember that blocs are not unique in American life, nor are they inherently evil. Their purposes determine their moral quality. In past years, labor, farmers, businessmen, veterans, and various national minorities have voted as blocs on various issues, and many still do. If the objectives are good, and each issue is decided on its own merits, a bloc is a wholesome force on the political scene. Negroes are, in fact, already voting spontaneously as a bloc. They voted overwhelmingly for President Kennedy, and before that for President Roosevelt. Development as a conscious bloc would give them more flexibility, more bargaining power, more clarity and more responsibility in assessing candidates and programs. Moreover a deeper involvement as a group in political life will bring them more independence. Consciously and creatively developed, political power may well, in the days to come, be the most effective new tool of the Negro's liberation.

Because Negroes can quite readily become a compact, conscious and vigorous force in politics, they can do more than achieve their own racial goals. American politics needs nothing so much as an injection of the idealism, self-sacrifice and sense of public service which is the hallmark of our movement. Until now, comparatively few major Negro leaders of talent and unimpeachable character have involved themselves actively in partisan politics. Such men as Judge William Hastie, Ralph Bunche, Benjamin Mays, A. Philip Randolph, to name but a few, have remained aloof from the political scene. In the coming period, they and many others must move out into political life as candidates and infuse it with their humanity, their honesty and their vision.

For whatever demands the Negro justly makes on his fellow citizens are not an effort to lift responsibility from himself. His tasks are still fundamental, involving risks and sacrifices which he has already proved himself prepared to make. In addition, he will have to learn new skills, new duties, and creatively and constructively to embrace a new way of life. Ask a prisoner released after years of confinement in jail what efforts he faces in taking on the privileges and responsibilities of freedom, and the enormity of the Negroes' task in the years ahead becomes clear.

VI

One aspect of the civil-rights struggle that receives little attention is the contribution it makes to the whole society. The Negro in winning rights for himself produces substantial benefits for the nation. Just as a doctor will occasionally reopen a wound, because a dangerous infection hovers beneath the half-healed surface, the revolution for human rights is opening up unhealthy areas in American life and permitting a new and wholesome healing to take place. Eventually the civil-rights movement will have contributed infinitely more to the nation than the eradication of racial injustice. It will have enlarged the concept of brotherhood to a vision of total interrelatedness. On that day, Canon John Donne's doctrine, "no man is an islande," will find its truest application in the United States.

In measuring the full implications of the civil-rights revolution, the greatest contribution may be in the area of world peace. The concept of nonviolence has spread on a mass scale in the United States as an instrument of change in the field of race relations. To date, only a relatively few practitioners of nonviolent direct action have been committed to its philosophy. The great mass have used it pragmatically as a tactical weapon, without being ready to live it.

More and more people, however, have begun to conceive of this powerful ethic as a necessary way of life in a world where the wildly accelerated development of nuclear power has brought into being weapons that can annihilate all humanity. Political agreements are no longer secure enough to safeguard life against a peril of such devastating finality. There must also be a philosophy, acceptable to the people, and stronger than resignation toward sudden death.

It is no longer merely the idealist or the doom-ridden who seeks for some controlling force capable of challenging the instrumentalities of destruction. Many are searching. Sooner or later all the peoples of the world, without regard to the political systems under which they live, will have to discover a way to live together in peace.

Man was born into barbarism when killing his fellow man was a normal condition of existence. He became endowed with a conscience. And he has now reached the day when violence toward another human being must become as abhorrent as eating another's flesh.

Nonviolence, the answer to the Negroes' need, may become the answer to the most desperate need of all humanity.

SELECTED BIBLIOGRAPHY

OTHER WORKS BY THE AUTHOR:

King, Martin Luther, Jr. *Stride Toward Freedom: The Montgomery Story.* Harper & Brothers, 1958.

———. *The Strength to Love.* Harper & Row, 1963.

———. *Where Do We Go from Here: Chaos or Community?* Harper & Row, 1967.

———. *The Trumpet of Conscience.* Harper & Row, 1967.

———. *A Testament of Hope.* James M. Washington, ed. HarperCollins Publishers, 1986.

FURTHER READING:

Ansbro, John. *Martin Luther King, Jr.: The Making of a Mind.* Orbis Books, 1982.

Bennett, Lerone, Jr. *What Manner of Man.* Johnson Publishing Co., 1968.

Branch, Taylor. *Parting the Waters: America in the King Years, 1954-1963.* Simon & Schuster, 1989.

Garrow, David. *Bearing the Cross: Martin Luther King, Jr.* W. W. Norton, 1981.

King, Coretta Scott. *My Life with Martin Luther King, Jr.* Holt, Rinehart, and Winston, 1969.

———. *The Words of Martin Luther King, Jr.* Newmarket Press, 1983.

Lewis, David L. *King: A Biography.* University of Illinois Press, 1970, 1978.

Oates, Stephen B. *Let the Trumpet Sound: The Life of Martin Luther King, Jr.* New American Library, 1982.

Reddick, Lawrence D. *Crusader Without Violence: A Biography of Martin Luther King, Jr.* Harper & Brothers, 1959.

Schulke, Flip, and Penelope O. McPhee. *King Remembered.* W. W. Norton, 1986.

INDEX